PERIODIC TABLE

A Cosmic Blueprint of Creation

SHIBU POTHEN

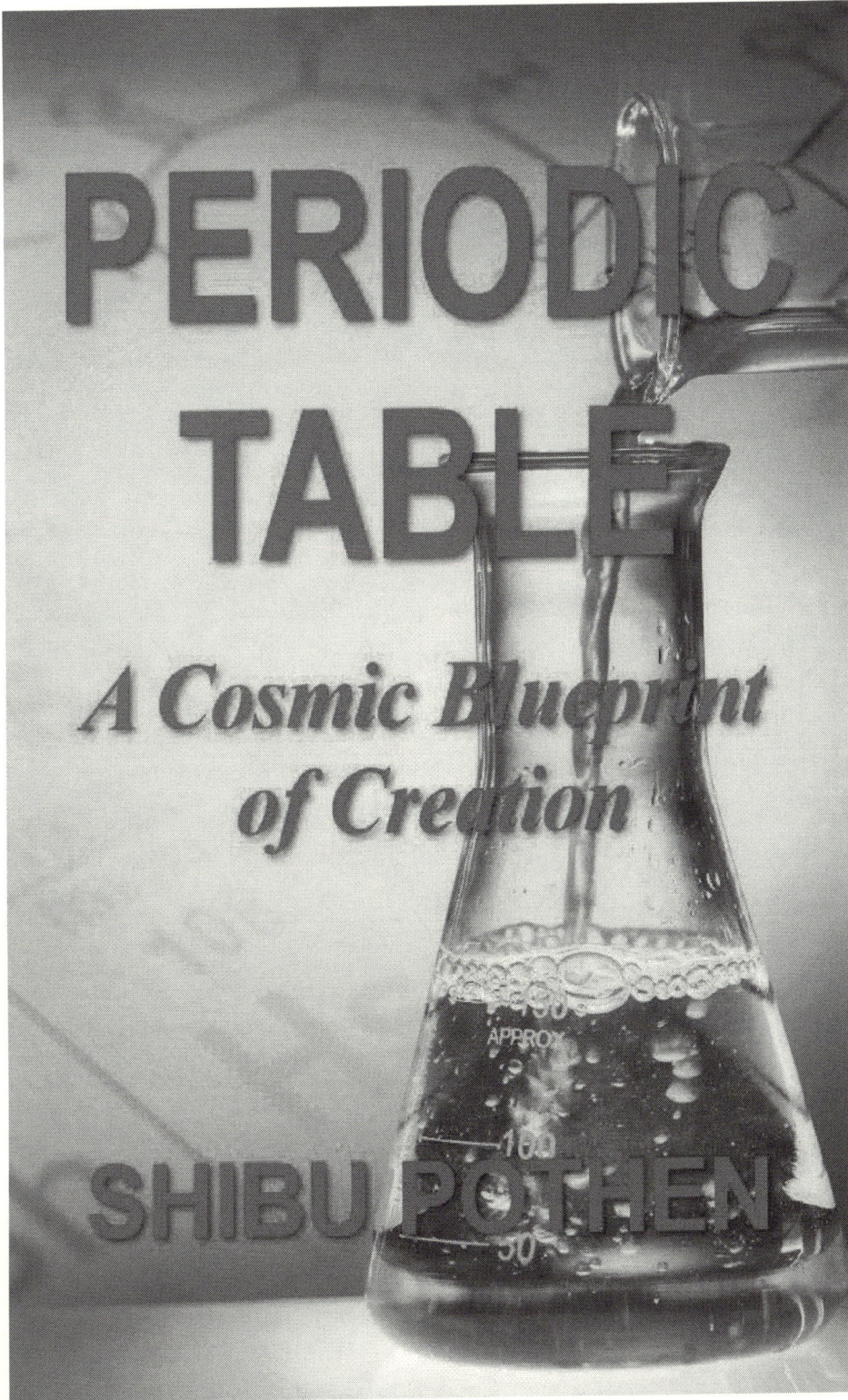

Contents

The author reflects the philosophy based on Psalm 68:11,
"The Lord gave the word and great was the company of those who published it."

This book is dedicated to my father, the late K. E. Pothen,
and my mother, Kunjamma Pothen.

Acknowledgements

This book has been in the making for about thirty-five years. I became interested in the periodic table when I was sixteen years old while attending Dhamtari Science College, in Dhamtari, India.

Now as this book is finished, I want to thank all those who contributed to it either directly or indirectly.

First I want to thank two chemists, Mr Jacob Koshy and Mr Abdul Gaffar, who encouraged me to study chemistry. Also I want to thank all my teachers who made me what I am today.

I want to thank my parents for their sacrifice and support. I also want to thank my sisters, Shirly and Sheela, and brothers-in-law, Johnson and James, for their support in many ways.

There are many people who were directly involved with the process of writing this book. Dr. Ravi Mishra, Dr. Shubhrata Mishra, Sophia Pothen, Jack Pothen and Mr. Prince Thomas helped me with their detailed comments. Finally, I thank my wife, Mariamma, and children, Sophia, Jack, Sara, Sam, and Sonel, for their cooperation.

Preface

I have always been fascinated by the biblical account of creation—the wonderful story of creating our beautiful universe and all of its complexity in seven days. Is that possible or is the biblical account a myth? In my search to know the truth, I focused my graduate studies in chemistry. Thus, I got the privilege to explore the cornerstone of chemistry—the periodic table. During my studies, I was astonished to see that various correlations exist between the Genesis version of creation and the periodic table. In this book, I give you the associations that exist between the Bible and the chemistry. There are many interesting connections I want to show to encourage further study and seek the significance of these parallels. The periodic table serves a deeper purpose than what meets the eye. It not effectively organizes the elements of the universe but also reveals the story of creation.

The periodic table is not just a chemical classification but is also a communication tool—it represents the only stable icon in this universe. It is a description of the elements that compose both the microscopic (atomic) and the macroscopic (cosmic) worlds. If an extraterrestrial being was to visit Earth, we would need to achieve a point of contact by finding something in common. As the elements are the same throughout the universe, it is logical that the periodic table would be that point of contact as it is the blueprint of the cosmos. Likewise, if God wanted to communicate with us, He would also use this cosmic blueprint. The periodic table is the cornerstone of communication and should be further studied to unlock the deeper meaning inherent in its design. By combining my interest in the periodic table and Genesis, I present to you a cosmic blueprint, a scientific approach in analysing the creation story. It is interesting to examine a deeper story contained within the periodic table. In this book, I will try to explain how the biblical account of creation parallels the scientific account of creation by the periodic table. Thus periodic table can be used to search further scientific interpretations of the Bible.

I want everyone to read this book to gain knowledge about relationships from both the fields and to make one's own educated judgment. I urge everyone to examine the book with an open mind and seek the deeper meaning. My belief is that the correlations in the book are just the tip of an iceberg showing a need for further research. We are living in a great time, very much equipped with modern technology and numerous resources at our fingertips. Thus, we also should apply the scientific method and use our resources to the utmost even to test our ideas and beliefs. My experience as a chemist has shown me that our studies of science and the scientific method can help in leading to a more sophisticated idea.

Why did a person like me, who had many years of educational background in the sciences, spend time on the Bible's account of creation? It started with Day 2. In 1912, Alfred Wegener found out that in the past, Earth was one supercontinent or Pangaea. Later in time, the continents were divided. Before this, no one nor no other literature or religious texts talked about a super continent. In Day 2, it talks about a supercontinent or Pangaea. The Bible says in Genesis 10:25 that during the times of Peleg, this supercontinent was divided into many continents. Because of this information, I took the Genesis account of creation seriously to see whether there was indeed a connection between science and the Bible.

I hope the book inspires more people to take up the search for the God and His works in the cosmic blueprint, the periodic table to new heights.

Thank you.

Introduction

Scientific enquiry is not the only way to understand the reality of the universe. We use science as it strives to be an unbiased medium to any culture. It is a noble way to understand the world in an objective and methodical manner. Chemistry points out the organization of cosmos. Therefore, I have attempted to understand the reality of the universe and our place in this grand system using chemistry. Moreover, chemistry is the oldest branch of science. It started when men used fire to cook tastier food. And a new culture of experiment for different cuisine is started thousands of years ago in caves and that spirit of experiment remains intact still today in those caves now known as chemical laboratories. Thousands of years before Aristotle, people in Egypt used chemical means for embalming, metal work, dyeing, glass making, and these process got an official name, alchemy, which recognised the need for experimental verification of theories. And from this land of Egypt, Moses, the great alchemist, published the first periodic table in a story form. The alchemist of in those days, who were dealing with costly metals like gold, had no real wish to make their process to public as it may help their competitors, so they invented a secret language that made their text incomprehensible. Modern chemistry is a continuation of Egyptian alchemy because the tree of chemistry has its root in ancient alchemy. In 1661 Robert Boyle put chemistry on a firm scientific footing, and he replaced the term *alchemy* by chemistry. If anyone does not agree with me because alchemy had an angle of mystery in it, I humbly want to point out that chemistry had its phlogiston theory as fantasy runs in the family. Thousands of years after Moses, another *M* appeared on the earth who predicted the properties of elements that no one has ever seen. That magician was Dmitri Ivanovich Mendeleev, and mystery continues as Mendeleev got membership to the Academy of Art but not to the Academy of Sciences because his periodic table is the art of universe.

When we plan to build a house, the first thing we need to find an architect to develop a blueprint in which our imagination of the house translates into a form. I became surprised when I saw a blueprint of the universe in the creation account written in the first chapter of Genesis. Chemical elements are analogues to alphabets making the fundamental cosmos. They, in different combinations, form all simple and complex systems of the universe. The human imagination and thought process is one of the prime examples of the complexities attained by reaction of chemical elements, enabling man to decode or being always in the quest for understanding all fundamentals of nature. In another word, our imagination is the reflection of chemical combinations going inside our brain, or thinking is a chemical process. The elements are the building blocks of the universe, and any story of creation will be incomplete without them. All elements have specific characteristics, which enable them to be organized in a sequence of tabular nature known as the periodic table. Therefore, the periodic table is the blueprint of the universe. So, it is appropriate to decode the periodic table to gain a better understanding of the story of the Genesis in the Bible.

Chemistry and the periodic table are inseparable because

the periodic table forms the society of elements. As stated in the book *The Elements* by John Emsley,

> As long as the chemistry is studied there will be a periodic table. And even if someday we communicate with another part of the universe, we can be sure that one thing that both cultures will have in common is an ordered system of elements that will be instantly recognizable by both intelligent life-forms.

The reason for a consistent periodic table throughout the universe is that chemicals do not change their behavior in space and time. As the elements are the same throughout the universe, it is logical that the consistent periodic table would be that point of contact. Likewise, if God wanted to communicate with us, He would also use the periodic table. The elements would be the alphabet within the periodic table and forms the language to tell the story of the universe and the deeper meaning of reality. Considering that everything, on both the microscopic and macroscopic scale, is fundamentally composed of the elements, communication would occur from this common foundation. As the periodic table is the cornerstone of communication to nature, it should be further investigated to unlock the deeper meaning inherent in its structure. The aim of this book is to present a new way of viewing chemical relationship across the periodic table, which can help us to find a relationship with the creator. Dmitri Ivanovich Mendeleev, a Russian chemist, published the first periodic table in 1869. He was well known as the living encyclopedia of chemical elements by the peers of his days. In a dream, Mendeleev saw that when elements are placed in the increasing order of atomic weight, their properties repeated in a periodic interval. It has been one of the most iconic discoveries in science and remains unchallenged to date.

Astonishingly, a comprehensive study of the periodic table corresponds well to the story of the seven days of creation in the Bible. As chemistry is an experimental science, it is natural that numbers lag far behind in chemistry, for example, organic superconductors, organic ferromagnets are far beyond the capabilities of quantum chemistry. Thus the reader will find here a way to think about organizing known facts about molecular electronic structure of atoms into a coherent pattern and from this base to look into the origin of the universe. Dmitri Ivanovich Mendeleev observed that many natural phenomena exhibit a dependence of a periodic character. Thus, the phenomena such as day and night, the seasons of the year, and all kinds of vibrations exhibit variations of a periodic character dependent on time and space. Correlations between the days of creation and the periodic table are not merely accidental; instead, we can show them as built into the format of universe, indicating an intelligent creator. Hence, knowing the correlations brings a paradigm shift toward the story of creation in the Bible, which, otherwise, in a contemporary worldview, is not more than a myth for most people. Even many Christians find it hard to accept the creation story in Genesis as a fact. So decoding the periodic table alongside the creation story of Genesis makes an old saying alive that Earth and its inhabitants at the center of creation because we are the observer of this grand universe.

Genesis

The book of Genesis is the first book of the Five Books of Moses or Pentateuch. It contains the account of God's cosmic creation pattern. All these books of Moses, as well as portions of Genesis, show that Moses was a compiler of these early documents. It's a common belief that he wrote down the memorized oral history and traditions. The word *Genesis* means "origin" or "source," and Moses recorded whatever was given by God. The name *Moses* means "to deliver," which was just what God set him out to do— deliver the Lord's words to man.

The second book of Exodus tells how Moses made a dais beneath the mountain, where the Lord ordered him to imprint His solidarity towards man; he had made a covenant with him and also with Israel. It declares that man is not alone in this universe. It is said that Moses was there with the Lord for forty days and forty nights and that he did not take of bread or water. Exodus gives a detailed description of the environment during this period: "Now Mount Sinai was all in smoke because the lord descended upon it in fire; and its smoke ascended like the smoke of a furnace, and the whole mountain quaked violently" (Exodus 19:18, NASB). It is felt that Mount Sinai was turned into a vibrating conical flask of universal proportions with Moses witnessing fire, fragrance, smoke, and sound. In the midst of the vapors of flame, Moses beheld the hand of God, the ultimate chemist, and was handed over the cosmic blueprint or the periodic table in the form of story imaginable to the generations.

In Genesis, God is clearly declared as the creator of heaven and earth and the first being (the alpha and the omega). It is recorded in the Bible that God completed each day of His work in creation, concluding that it was good (Genesis 1:4–31). This implies that God took pleasure in His creation and created man as His final zenith of goodness, which pleased him greatly. After the creation of the man, God blessed them to be fruitful, multiply, fill the earth, subdue it, and have dominion over the fish of the sea and the birds of the air, and over every living thing that moves upon the earth (Genesis 1–28). Genesis is written as an authentic history and describes the lives of Abraham, Isaac, Jacob, and his twelve sons who were the ancestral heads of the twelve tribes of Israel. The Jewish people, from the earliest biblical times to the present day, have always regarded this portion of Genesis as the true record of their nation's history.

Our focus is the first eleven chapters of Genesis where creation and the beginnings of mankind are mentioned. These eleven chapters are the most criticized by modern scholars and scientists. Many postulate that the narrative of the creation in Genesis is a myth or simple symbolism for the Judaic and Christian faith. The links between Genesis and the periodic table is illustrated in the chapters ahead, which will convey that Genesis is consistent with modern science. There is a further need of reinterpretation of the book of Genesis to align it with today's scientific knowledge. If there are any new unexplored elements that man has been contemplating based on known knowledge, it may be that Genesis can provide clues for our search. The biblical works of Genesis have found strength in recent theories like the big bang theory, and there are many yet to be found. My work seeks to open our minds such that we may further explore the books of the Bible in order to seek a better understanding of the universe.

Scientific Aspects of the Book of Genesis

The Hebrew meaning of Genesis is the "book of commencements." There are various novel openings of the universe recorded in Genesis. The book of Genesis starts with God as the creator. There are seven periods of creation recorded in the beginning of Genesis, with each commencement interpreted as a "day." In Hebrew scripture, the word *yom* is translated as "day," which simply means "a period of time with a discrete beginning and ending." According to Genesis, the sun, moon, and stars did not appear until the fourth "day"; thus, it's implausible that this day refers to a solar day. In Genesis, God created the world in six days and consecrates the seventh after giving mankind his first commandment: "be fruitful and reproduce." It says that God marked the world as "very good," but it then became corrupted by the sin of man, and God sent a great flood to destroy it, saving only the righteous (Noah and his family). It is recorded in Genesis 7:1 that the Lord ordered Noah to go into the ark with his whole family because God found them to be righteous in that generation. Afterward, the world was repopulated from the family of Noah (Hebrews 11:7, Genesis 5:22).

The world and its every living and non-living thing are composed of many elements. In chemistry, it is the valence electrons in the outermost shell of an atom that participate in all of the chemical reactions of that element. Thus, the valence electrons represent the combining capacity, or valency, of an element and function as the preserver of the atom, just as in the book of Genesis that God is the creator and preserver of the universe. God has the exclusive decisive power of the universe but is distinct from it. Similarly, all of the elements are spread all over the universe, but it is still a mystery as to how the Z and W boson particles of atoms are made or from where they originate. The universe, the elements, and God's creation are all collectively linked. The periodic table explains the deep connection with the book of Genesis.

Correlation between Genesis and Periodic Table					
Days of Genesis	Creation by God	Main Groups	Elements According Groups	Periods	Elements According Period
First	Light (Day and Night) and Water	IA	H, Li, Na, K, Rb, Cs, Fr	1	H and He
Second	Heavens and Sky through separation of water	IIA and IIIA	Be, Mg, Ca, Sr, Ba, Ra and B, Al, Ga, In, Tl, Nh	2	Li, Be, B, C, N, O, F, Ne
Third	Separated land from sea and production of vegetation	IVA	C, Si, Ge, Sn, Pb, Fl	3	Na, Mg, Al, Si, P, S, Cl, Ar
Fourth	Sun, Moon, and stars.	VA	N, P, As, Sb, Bi, Mc	4	K, Ca, Sc, Ti, V, Cr, Mn, Fe, Co, Ni, Cu, Zn, Ga, Ge, As, Se, Br, Kr
Fifth	Creatures of the sea and the birds to fly across the heavens	VIA	O, S, Se, Te, Po, Lv	5	Te Rb, Sr, Y, Zr, Nb, Mo, Tc, Ru, Rh, Pd, Ag, Cd, In, Sn, Sb, I, Xe
Sixth	Wild beasts, livestock, and reptiles and human beings	VIIA	F, Cl, Br, I, At, Ts	6	Cs, Ba, La, Hf, Ta, W, Re, Os, Ir, Pt, Au, Hg, Tl, Pb, Bi, Po, At, Rn, **Lanthanides**
Seventh	Creation is completed and God rested from all His work.	VIIIA	He, Ne, Ar, Kr, Xe, Rn, Og	7	Fr, Ra, Ac, Rf, Db, Sg, Bh, Hs, Mt, Ds, Rg, Cn, Nh, Fl, Mc, Lv, Ts, Og, **Actinides**

According to Genesis, eight acts of creation were done over six days with a concluding seventh day. Surprisingly, each day of creation by God as described in the book of Genesis is very much linked to the respective group members, particularly with the representative elements of each family group. The groups, or families, of the periodic table represent the days of God's creation. Characteristics and the special uses of elements of the groups, particularly

18

the representative element of each family, resemble the seven days of creation. Within the first three days, there were three different acts of division: on the first day, the darkness was separated from light; on the second day, the "waters above" from the "waters below"; and on the third day, the sea from the land. Thus, these three days of creation are days of separation. The first three periods of the periodic table also show gaps between the groups, confirming the separation. In the next three days, these previous divisions are settled with non-living and living creations. For example, on the fourth day, the darkness and light was settled with the sun, moon, and stars. In the fifth day, the seas and skies was settled with fish and birds. Finally, on the sixth day, land-based creatures and humankind settled on the land.

It is very surprising that each period and each group of the periodic table represents each day of creation by God. The properties of each element of the periodic table resemble the theme of seven creation days. This correlation between them is shown in the above chart.

Elements

Elements are the foundation of the universe. All material things in the universe are composed of different combinations of known elements. An element is a substance made from only one type of atom. For example, the element hydrogen has atoms containing just one proton and one electron. Every atom of each element has a distinct number of positively charged protons in a central nucleus encircled by an equal number of negatively charged electrons. Thus, an atom is electrically neutral. The nucleus may also contain a variable number of neutrons, giving rise to various isotopes of the element. So, a chemical element is a pure chemical substance comprising a single type of atom distinguished by its atomic number that is further defined by the number of protons in its atomic nucleus. Atomic mass is the mass of protons, neutrons, and electrons in an atom. The atomic number, representing the number of protons, is unique to a particular element. No two elements have the same atomic number. All elements display two types of properties, chemical and physical. The chemical property of an element is expressed through chemical reactions whereas the physical properties of the element are observable in its pure form at standard conditions. The chemical properties of an element are dependent on the distribution of electrons around its nucleus. The outer or valence electrons play a major role in any chemical reaction but doesn't affect the nucleus. Thus, the atomic number remains unchanged in a chemical reaction, thereby preserving the identity of the element. According to their properties, elements are classified into metals, metalloids, and non-metals. There are ninety-two naturally occurring chemical elements in the Earth. All entities in the universe are the result of chemical reactions among combinations of atoms of different elements. It is believed that most comprehensive matter found in stars and interstellar clouds is in the form of atoms or ions. Hydrogen is the most abundant element in the known universe with helium as the second most, produced by the big bang.

At any given moment, the elements are changing, moving, and expanding in the universe. Thus, they play a vital role in modifying and developing the world. All elements give balance and structure to the world and its living bodies. The philosophy behind using elements for direction of creation is due to the fact that the entire universe is composed of them in various combinations. We can imagine that the periodic table illustrates the universe filled with various types of elements.

Periodic Table

History

The modern periodic table is the most systematic way of listing the chemical elements. It is a tabular compilation, arranged in rows and columns, organized on the basis of atomic number, electronic configuration, and chemical properties. Each row in the table is a period with a total of seven periods. Each period has elements with the same number of electron energy levels with respect to the period number. The number of occupied energy levels is the same when moving across each period from left to right, and the energy level gradually becomes filled with electrons. On the left-hand side of the table, the highest occupied energy level has only one electron. The physical and chemical properties of the elements rotate in a cyclic fashion from left to right. Similarly, a column of the periodic table is known as a group with a total of eighteen groups present. The arrangement of elements in a column is from top to down based on the increasing number of energy levels. Elements in a group or column are similar with respect to their chemical and physical properties as they share the same number of valence electrons. Thus, all elements have a different period and group.

The periodic table was first published in the year 1869 by the Russian chemistry professor Dmitri Ivanovich Mendeleev. He developed the table by arranging the elements according to their atomic weight. Mendeleev is accredited for his efforts in rearranging the elements in a systematic way based on periodic trends. His periodic table also predicted the properties of yet-to-be-discovered unknown elements based on his formula. Later these predictions were proved with the discovery of new elements. Mendeleev published the periodic table in his preliminary work, *Principles of Chemistry*, in 1872. He arranged his table with the sixty-five known elements. It was later modified and extended to accommodate new elements. He arranged the elements in horizontal rows and vertical columns of a table in the order of their increasing atomic weights in such a way that the elements with similar properties occupied the same vertical column called group. Mendeleev realized that his table would be very useful in chemistry and left spaces for elements yet to be discovered. However, Mendeleev also plotted some elements out of the strict weight sequence arrangement to better match their properties with neighboring elements. He corrected the values of several atomic masses and predicted the existence and properties of a few new elements in the empty cells of his table. There were some shortcomings to Mendeleev's table as he could not to make predictions about noble gasses and could not find one specific place for hydrogen. Mendeleev's work was soon corrected and enhanced by the discovery of atomic number by Henry Moseley.

In the year 1914, an English physicist by the name of Henry Moseley developed a way to study atomic structure with X-ray spectra, resulting in the correct positioning of elements in the periodic table by correlating wavelength to atomic number. Prior to this discovery, elements were arranged by their atomic weight. Moseley changed the sequence in periodic table according to atomic number. His discoveries resulted in a more accurate positioning of elements in the periodic table. Moseley's work with the atomic number is the basis of the modern periodic table.

An Information Grid

The periodic table is universal in the discipline of chemistry, giving a concise efficient outline for classifying and systematizing different forms of chemical properties. The power of the periodic table lies in its ability to predict+ new elements and their properties. It tells the chemical properties of an element based on its place on the table. There are also widespread applications of the table in physics, biology, engineering, and industry. As of now, there are 118 elements in the standard periodic table. In printed versions of the periodic tables, each element is listed with its element symbol and atomic number. There are 94 elements found on Earth. The rest of the elements are synthetic, or artificially produced in particle accelerators. Elements like technetium (43), promethium (61), neptunium (93), and plutonium (94) have no stable isotopes. Isotopes are variants of a particular chemical element, which differ in atomic weight due to different number of neutrons; however, all isotopes of an element have the same number of protons in each atom. In small amounts, their traces can be found on earth as products of natural radioactive decay processes.

The periodic table provides an abundance of information such as abbreviated electron configuration, electro-negativity, and valence numbers. There are many forms of the periodic table used in chemistry other than Mendeleev's table. These are the short periodic table, long periodic table, Hull periodic table, and the modern periodic table. The short periodic table itemize elements known by 1930 and in the modern short form; the lanthanides and actinides are not shown. Thorium (90), protactinium (91), and uranium (92) were placed in groups IVB, VB, and VIB respectively, because of their similarities to hafnium (72), tantalum (73), and tungsten (74). The short form of the periodic table is based on the chemical properties; the long form of the table became popular because it explains the atomic structures of the elements. This form brings out the different series of elements corresponding to the filling of the different kinds of the electron shell.

Periodic Table (Short Form)

| I | | II | | III | | IV | | V | | VI | | VII | | VIII | 0 |
a	b	a	b	a	b	a	b	a	b	a	b	a	b		g
^{1}H						^{1}H						^{1}H			^{2}He
^{3}Li		^{4}Be		^{5}B		^{6}C		^{7}N		^{8}O		^{9}F			^{10}Ne
^{11}Na		^{12}Mg		^{13}Al		^{14}Si		^{15}P		^{16}S		^{17}Cl			^{18}Ar
^{19}K	^{29}Cu	^{20}Ca	^{30}Zn	^{31}Ga	^{21}Sc	^{32}Ge	^{22}Ti	^{33}As	^{23}V	^{34}Se	^{24}Cr	^{35}Br	^{25}Mn	^{26}Fe,^{27}Co,^{28}Ni	^{36}Kr
^{37}Rb	^{47}Ag	^{38}Sr	^{48}Cd	^{49}In	^{39}Y	^{50}Sn	^{40}Zr	^{51}Sb	^{41}Nb	^{52}Te	^{42}Mo	^{53}I	^{43}Tc	^{44}Ru,^{45}Rh,^{46}Pd	^{54}Xe
^{55}Cs	^{79}Au	^{56}Ba	^{80}Hg	^{81}Tl	57-71*	^{82}Pb	^{72}Hf	^{83}Bi	^{73}Ta	^{84}Po	^{74}W	^{85}At	^{75}Re	^{76}Os,^{77}Ir,^{78}Pt	^{86}Rn
^{87}Fr	^{111}Rg	^{88}Ra	^{112}Cn	^{113}Nh	89-103*	^{114}Fl	^{104}Rf	^{115}Mc	^{105}Db	^{116}Lv	^{106}Sg	^{117}Ts	^{107}Bh	^{108}Hs,^{109}Mt,^{110}Ds	^{118}Og

The long form periodic table has many advantages over the short form, but it lost the secondary relationships, which are better shown in the short form. I. D. Margary formulated Hull periodic table in 1921, a modified form of the table suggested by T. Bayley in 1882.

The Hull table is a compromise between the long form and the short form as it shows both the atomic structure and secondary relationships.

The history of the periodic table began with the publication of the first periodic table by Dmitri Mendeleev in 1869. Although Mendeleev had made the historic discovery, he could not progress further because new elements were discovered later. The further development in the periodic table was restricted until Bohr model of the atom had been formulated. In 1913 Henry Moseley showed that it is the atomic number that is the most fundamental to the chemical properties of the elements. Like Mendeleev, Moseley was able to predict the existence of new elements based on his work. He brought changes to Mendeleev's periodic law, arranging the elements in order of increasing atomic number, which is currently used. Mosley established the Modern Periodic Law, which states that the physical and chemical properties of the elements are periodic functions of their atomic numbers.

Due to the Periodic Law, chemists strived to discover new elements and added more than fifty-three elements after Mendeleev published his first periodic table.

Modern Periodic Table

Groups and Periods of Periodic Table

Elements are arranged in the periodic table by periods and groups. The rows are arranged so that elements with similar characteristics fall into the same vertical columns called groups or families. The number of electrons in any element's outer shell is the same as the number of its group in the periodic table. Groups have elements with the same outer electron arrangement. Elements located in the same group keep the same number of valence electrons. As a result of containing the same number of valence electrons, elements in a group share similar but not identical chemical characteristics. Each horizontal row in the table is known as period. In Mendeleev's original table, each period was of the same length. The number of elements in a period increases from top to down as more orbitals are added. Thus, modern tables acquire progressively longer periods further down the table. The elements in the period are not alike in properties; in fact, the properties change greatly across in a given row. The first element in a period is always an extremely active solid while the last element in a period is always a noble gas, which is chemically inert.

Vertically into Groups or Families
Horizontally into Periods

Families on Periodic Table

There are two categories of groups or families—A and B. The group A elements are the main group elements. Their placement is under main eight groups such as IA, IIA, IIIA, IVA, VA, VIA, VIIA, Zero Group. The remaining elements of group B include in the groups IIIB, IVB, VB, VIB, VIIB, VIII, VIII, VIII, IB, and IIB, known as the transition elements. Each group is named by a particular element of the same family. Thus, IA, IIA, IIIA, IVA, VA, VIA, VIIA, VIIIA groups are also known as the family of alkali metals, alkaline earth metals, boron, carbon, nitrogen, oxygen, halogen, and the noble gases, respectively. An electron configuration illustrates the number of electrons in each orbital in a specific atom. These electron configurations of elements exhibit that the number of valence electrons matches with group number. The IA family has 1 valence electron; similarly, the IIA family has 2, the III A family has 3, the IVA family has 4, the VA family has 5, the VIA family has 6, the VIIA family has 7, and the Zero Group

29

family has 8 valence electrons.

The periodic table groups are as follows (the old systems are shown in the brackets: American):

- Group 1 (IA): the alkali metals or lithium family
- Group 2 (IIA): the alkaline earth metals or beryllium family
- Group 3 (IIIB): the scandium family
- Group 4 (IVB): the titanium family
- Group 5 (VB): the vanadium family
- Group 6 (VIB): the chromium family
- Group 7 (VIIB): the manganese family
- Group 8 (VIII): the iron family
- Group 9 (VIII): the cobalt family
- Group 10 (VIII): the nickel family
- Group 11 (IB): the coinage metals (not an IUPAC recommended name) or copper family
- Group 12 (IIB): the zinc family
- Group 13 (IIIA): the boron family
- Group 14 (IVA): the carbon family
- Group 15 (VA): the pnictogens or nitrogen family
- Group 16 (VIA): the chalcogens or oxygen family
- Group 17 (VIIA): the halogens or fluorine family
- Group 18 (Group O): the noble gases or helium family

Group 1: Family of alkali metals or lithium

The alkali metals are placed in Group IA (first column) of the periodic table. Alkali metals form salts and numerous compounds and are less dense than other metals. Their ions form a +1 charge and have the largest atom sizes of all the elements in their periods. These metals are extremely reactive.

Group 2: Family of alkaline earth metals or beryllium

The alkaline earth metals are placed in Group IIA (second column) of the periodic table. Many compounds are formed by these metals. They have ions with a +2 charge. Their atoms are smaller than those of the alkali metals.

Groups 3–12: Transition metals

The transition elements are in groups 3 to 12. Iron and gold are well known transition metals. They form positively charged ions.

Groups 13: Boron family

Boron and aluminum are found on Earth; the rest of the elements are found in very minute amount.

Group 14: Carbon family

Include some metals, some metalloids, and some nonmetals.

Groups 15 Nitrogen Family

The nitrogen family is also called pnictogen. It includes some metals, some metalloids, and some nonmetals.

Group 16: Oxygen family

The Oxygen family are also called the chalcogens. The

elements of this family are found in both free and combined states

Group 17: The halogens family

Elements of Group 17 are known as the halogens. Halogens are non-metals and form ions with a -1 charge. Fluorine is the most electronegative element of the entire periodic table. The halogens are highly reactive. All halogens form acids with hydrogen as hydrofluoric acid, hydrochloric acid, etc. Halogens are commonly found in bleaches, disinfectants, and salts.

Group 18: The noble gases or helium family/neon family

The elements of Group 18 are known as the noble gases. The noble gases are nonreactive because their valence shell is filled with electrons. Neon and helium are the most inert elements among the noble gases. The reactivity of the gases increases as the periods increase because heavier noble gases have much larger electron shells. The reactivity of noble gases remains very low in absolute terms. Noble gases are used in lasers, lighted signs, and refrigerants.

Rare Earth Elements

The rare earth elements are divided into the lanthanides (elements 58–71) and the actinides (elements 90–103). Rare earth elements occur naturally on earth in very small quantities.

Lanthanides

The fourteen elements of the sixth period of the periodic table, which has atomic numbers following lanthanum, are called the lanthanides. The lanthanides are silvery metals that discolor easily. They are relatively soft metals, and their melting and boiling points are high. Cerium, lanthanum, neodymium, and praseodymium are the most common lanthanides found in minerals. These elements are generally used in lamps, magnets, and lasers as well as for improving the properties of other metals.

Actinides

The actinides are in the row below the lanthanides. They follow actinium for their atomic numbers. All actinides are radioactive with positively charged ions. These are reactive metals and form compounds with most nonmetals. The actinides are mainly used in medicines and nuclear devices.

Synthetic Elements

Rutherfordium (Rf): Rutherfordium is a highly radioactive chemical element. Out of nine known isotopes, Rf^{265} is the most stable one with a half-life of about thirteen hours. Rutherfordium prefers oxidation state IV and compounds such as $RfOCl_2$ are confirmed. Rutherfordium is a synthetic element.

Dubnium (Db): Dubnium has nine known isotopes. Its longest-lived isotope is $Dubnium^{268}$ with a half-life of thirty-two hours.

Seaborgium (Sg): Seaborgium is an artificially produced radioactive chemical element. Its appearance is unknown but it may be a silvery white or metallic grey color. The most stable isotope Sg^{271} has a half-life of 2.4 minutes. The little research that has been carried out on seaborgium's chemistry suggests that it prefers oxidation state VI and forms a compound SgO_2Cl_2.

Bohrium (Bh): Bohrium is an artificially produced radioactive element. It is probably silvery or metallic grey. It's most stable isotope, Bh^{262}, has a half-life of seventeen seconds.

Hassium (Hs): Hassium is a synthetic chemical element. Its chemical properties are similar to those of osmium with a silvery white or metallic grey color and a half-life of 9.7 seconds.

Meitnerium (Mt): Meitnerium has been not researched chemically. It is expected to be similar to other elements of group 9 such as iridium. The half-life of meitnerium is about 3.8 milliseconds.

Darmstadtium (Ds): Darmstadtium is a synthetic element which quickly decays. Its isotopes of atomic weights 279–281 have half-lives measured in microseconds.

Darmstadtium has a half-life of about 0.1 milliseconds.

Roentgenium (Rg): The position of Rg in the periodic table is in group 11 below gold. Thus, it is estimated that this element should possess similar physical properties but like gold may be loath to make them. Its appearance is said to be yellow or orange metallic (like gold).

Copernicium (Cn): The position of Cn in the periodic table is in group 12. It is placed below mercury and should have the physical properties of a heavy metal. It may be possible for it to have two kinds of chemistry, corresponding to oxidation states M(I) and M(II). The latter form is more unstable. If the periodic trends are followed, it is expected to be a liquid metal more volatile than mercury. A half-life of Cn is about 0.24 milliseconds.

Nihonium (Nh): In 2004, Japanese scientists declared

that they succeeded in synthesising the element. Its atomic number is 113 and was created by bombarding a target of bismuth^{-209} with accelerated nuclei of zinc^{70} and detected a single atom of the Nihonium. It is expected to have properties similar of thallium and indium.

Flerovium (Fl): Flerovium is a superheavy artificial chemical element with symbol Fl and atomic number 114. The properties of Flerovium are expected to be similar to those of lead and tin. Flerovium can be synthesised by bombarding plutonium^{244} with calcium^{48} heavy beams. Fl has a half-life of about 21 seconds.

Moscovium (Mc): Moscovium is an artificially produced radioactive chemical element with symbol Mc and an atomic number of 115. It was discovered when Americium^{243} atoms were bombarded with calcium^{48} ions. Four atoms of moscovium were produced that decayed into atoms of nihonium in less than one-tenth second. Its position in the periodic table is in group 15, below bismuth. This should have the physical properties of a heavy metal, and it should be possible to have two kinds of chemistry, corresponding to oxidation states M(III) and M(V). The former form is more stable.

Livermorium (Lv): Livermorium is a synthetic superheavy element with symbol Lv and atomic number 116. In 1999, researchers at Lawrence Berkeley National Laboratory announced the discovery of elements 116. Due to its position in the periodic table, it is expected to have properties similar to those of polonium and tellurium.

Tennessine (Ts): Tennessine was first synthesized in 2010 by a joint team of Russian and American scientists at the Joint Institute for Nuclear Research (JINR) in Dubna, Russia, and has the atomic number 117.

Oganesson (Og): Oganesson was first synthesized in 2002 by a joint team of Russian and American scientists at the Joint Institute for Nuclear Research (JINR) in Dubna, Russia, and has the atomic number 118. Oganesson would probably share the properties of its group of the noble gases. It resembles radon in its chemical properties.

Periods on Periodic Table

Periodic table has seven periods as follows:

Period 1:

This period contains two elements: Hydrogen and Helium.

Period 2:

The second period contains eight elements: Lithium, Beryllium, Boron, Carbon, Nitrogen, Oxygen, Fluorine, and Neon

Period 3:

The third period contains eight elements: Sodium, Magnesium, Aluminium, Silicon, Phosphorus, Sulphur, Chlorine, and Argon

Period 4:

This fourth period contains eighteen elements: Potassium, Calcium, Scandium, Titanium, Vanadium, Chromium, Manganese, Iron, Cobalt, Nickel, Copper, Zinc, Gallium, Germanium, Arsenic, Selenium, and Bromine

Period 5:

This period contains eighteen elements: Rubidium, Strontium, Yttrium, Zirconium, Niobium, Molybdenum, Technetium, Ruthenium, Rhodium, Palladium, Silver, Cadmium, Indium, Tin, Antimony, Tellurium, Iodine, and Xenon

Period 6:

This period contains thirty-two elements: Caesium, Barium, 14 Lanthanides, Lutetium, Hafnium, Tantalum, Tungsten, Rhenium, Osmium, Iridium, Platinum, Gold, Mercury, Thallium, Lead, Bismuth, Polonium, Astatine, and Radon

Period 7:

This period contains thirty-two elements, but there are only three primordial elements: Thorium, Uranium, and Plutonium.

The elements of f-block are consigned to the two periods in periodic table namely Period-6 (lanthanides) and Period-7 (actinides) since that is where they are located in the full, or extended, version of the periodic table.

The elements can be split into metals and nonmetals. Metals comprise more than seventy five percent of all known elements and appear on the left side of the periodic table. Usually, metals are solid in nature at room temperature. Mercury is an exceptional metal because it is liquid at room temperature. Metals have high melting and boiling points, with tungsten having the highest melting point 3422°C. Gallium and caesium are also exceptional metals as they have very low melting points at 29°C and

28°C, respectively. Metals are also good conductors of heat and electricity.

Metals are placed on the left-hand side of the periodic table. When a metal is malleable, it can be flattened into thin sheets via hammering. Being ductile means metals can be molded into wires. Nonmetals are placed at the top right-hand side of the periodic table. So the property of elements in horizontal row changes from metallic on the left to nonmetallic on the right. Nonmetals are either solids or gases at room temperature with low melting and boiling points but boron and carbon have a high melting point due to the formation of covalent bond in their crystal structure. Nonmetals are poor conductors of heat and electricity.

Most of the nonmetals are hard and neither malleable nor ductile. The elements with the characteristics of both metals and nonmetals are called metalloids. Silicon and germanium are examples of metalloids. The metalloids show specific variations on boiling and melting points and densities. Good semiconductors being made up of metalloids. The metalloids are placed along the transverse line between the metals and non-metals in the periodic table.

First Day of Creation and the Periodic Table

First day of creation in Genesis 1:1–5, NKJV:

> [1]In the beginning God created the heavens and the earth. [2]The earth was without form, and void; and darkness was on the face of the deep. And the Spirit of God was hovering over the face of the waters.
> [3]Then God said, "Let there be light"; and there was light. [4]And God saw the light, that it was good; and God divided the light from the darkness. [5]God called the light Day, and the darkness He called Night. So the evening and the morning were the first day.

Genesis starts with God's creation account of heavens and earth on the first day. However, the first day's most important event is the separation of light from darkness marking the beginning of all creation. The prevailing scientific theory of the beginning of the universe is the big bang. It occurred over 13.8 billion years ago, which would have lightened up the universe. All the light we see today is due to the burning up of stars. They undergo nuclear processes and radiate light until death. A comparison of the day with the periodic table illustrate that the elements of the first period and the group have characteristics that relate them to light.

Periodic Table
(First Period and First Group)
and First Day of Genesis

	IA																		0

Group →

Period	IA	IIA											IIIA	IVA	VA	VIA	VIIA	0
1	H		SEPARATION BETWEEN DARKNESS AND LIGHT															He
2	Li	Be											B (5)	C (6)	N (7)	O (8)	F (9)	Ne (10)
3	Na	Mg (12)	IIIB	IVB	VB	VIB	VIIB	VIII			IB	IIB	Al (13)	Si (14)	P (15)	S (16)	Cl (17)	Ar (18)
4	K	Ca (20)	Sc (21)	Ti (22)	V (23)	Cr (24)	Mn (25)	Fe (26)	Co (27)	Ni (28)	Cu (29)	Zn (30)	Ga (31)	Ge (32)	As (33)	Se (34)	Br (35)	Kr (36)
5	Rb	Sr (38)	Y (39)	Zr (40)	Nb (41)	Mo (42)	Tc (43)	Ru (44)	Rh (45)	Pd (46)	Ag (47)	Cd (48)	In (49)	Sn (50)	Sb (51)	Te (52)	I (53)	Xe (54)
6	Cs	Ba (56)	La (57)	Hf (72)	Ta (73)	W (74)	Re (75)	Os (76)	Ir (77)	Pt (78)	Au (79)	Hg (80)	Tl (81)	Pb (82)	Bi (83)	Po (84)	At (85)	Rn (86)
7	Fr	Ra (88)	Ac (89)	Rf (104)	Db (105)	Sg (106)	Bh (107)	Hs (108)	Mt (109)	Ds (110)	Rg (111)	Cn (112)	Nh (113)	Fl (114)	Mc (115)	Lv (116)	Ts (117)	Og (118)

La (57)	Ce (58)	Pr (59)	Nd (60)	Pm (61)	Sm (62)	Eu (63)	Gd (64)	Tb (65)	Dy (66)	Ho (67)	Er (68)	Tm (69)	Yb (70)	Lu (71)
Ac (89)	Th (90)	Pa (91)	U (92)	Np (93)	Pu (94)	Am (95)	Cm (96)	Bk (97)	Cf (98)	Es (99)	Fm (100)	Md (101)	No (102)	Lr (103)

First Day in Periods

The structural design of the periodic table's first period has a huge separation reminding of the creation's first-day separation of light from darkness. The first period consists of only two elements, hydrogen and helium. Hydrogen was the first element produced in the universe along with some traces of helium and lithium. These three elements in the beginning also remind of the triune God.

The elements of the first period are the most abundant in the universe, as per current estimation hydrogen fill out

40

73% and helium 25% of the universe. Hydrogen is the simplest atom of all, consisting of a single proton with a single electron around its orbit. It is found in great abundance in stars and gas giant planets. It provides dynamic power to stars through proton-proton reactions and CNO cycle nuclear fusion. Fusion is a nuclear reaction in which two or more atomic nuclei collide at rapid speeds joining to form a new nucleus. During this process, matter is not conserved as some of the matter of the fusing nuclei is converted to energy. All the heat and light from the stars are generated through the fusion process. Due to high temperature in stars, hydrogen is found in the fourth state of matter called plasma, where hydrogen is ionised with equal number of proton and electron, causing high electrical conductivity to produce light. In the interstellar medium, it is always in the neutral atomic state. Hydrogen gas is highly flammable. Helium is the second most abundant element in the universe. All of the helium in the universe is created from the fusion of hydrogen atoms, either in the early universe or in stars. Most stars, after converting a significant portion of their hydrogen to helium, undergo an internal change. The internal core of the star collapses and heats up to a point where helium fuses into larger atoms. The fusion of hydrogen into helium can take place only under high temperature and density. It begins when two protons smash together strong enough to overcome the mutual repulsion caused by their positive electric charges and unite under the strong force, which functions in a short range. The protons emit a positive charge in the form of a positron, which collides with normal electron to generate energy as gamma rays. The transformation creates a deuterium nucleus and a minute particle called a neutrino. Fusion of the deuterium with another proton produces a light form of helium, He^3. When two He^3 atoms fuses into a normal helium atom with two protons and two neutrons, it completes the fusion process. Every step in this reaction generates heat and light, due to slight loss of mass.

As stated in the book *The Elements* by Theodore Gray,

> Stars shine because they are transmuting vast amount of hydrogen into helium. Our sun alone consumes six hundred million tons of hydrogen per second, converting it into five hundred and ninety-six million tons of helium. And where do the other four million tons per second go? It's converted into energy according to Einstein's famous formula, $E=mc^2$.

Hydrogen is the light makerof the universe since the beginning itself and makes them part of the first day of creation in the book of Genesis.

First Day in Group

Group IA has seven elements namely hydrogen (H), lithium (Li), sodium (Na), potassium (K), rubidium (Rb), caesium (Cs),and francium (Fr). Hydrogen (H) is the first element of Group IA but seldom exhibits similar behavior with the other alkali metals of its group. Hydrogen loses an electron to make a positive ion, a property of metals, but, it can also gain an electron to form a negative ion, like nonmetals. Except for hydrogen, the remaining elements Li, Na, K, Rb, Cs, and Fr are considered alkali metals. These particular elements were given the name *alkali*

42

because they react with water to form hydroxide ions, creating a basic solution. Alkali metals are highly reactive metals. These metals are extremely soft and bright silver in color. They also have low boiling points, melting points, and density than most elements.

Sodium and potassium are the most abundant Group IA elements on the earth. These occur in salt deposits in rock, formed from salt water evaporating from other elements. Lithium, rubidium, and caesium are found in much lower amounts. Among the Group IA elements, francium is radioactive. All known alkali metals of Group IA found in nature. This group lies in the s-block of the periodic table as all alkali metals have their outermost electron in an s-orbital.

All alkali metals react vigorously with cold water to form an aqueous solution of the strongly basic alkali metal hydroxide and release hydrogen gas. This reaction becomes more vigorous going down the group. Lithium reacts steadily with fizziness while other alkali metals like sodium and potassium ignite. Rubidium and caesium reacts in water and generate immense hydrogen gas so rapidly that shock waves formed in the water, which can shatter glass containers. An alkali metal produces an explosion in two separate stages. In the first stage, metal reacts with the water and breaks hydrogen bonds, releasing hydrogen gas. Second, the heat generated by the reaction often ignites the hydrogen gas; as a result, hydrogen burns and visible flame appears above the bowl of water.

The chemical reaction of the alkali metals with water is:

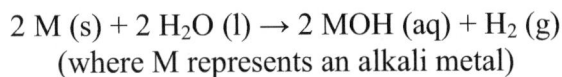

$$2 \text{ M (s)} + 2 \text{ H}_2\text{O (l)} \rightarrow 2 \text{ MOH (aq)} + \text{H}_2 \text{ (g)}$$
(where M represents an alkali metal)

Furthermore, alkali metals have their own particular

43

flame colors. The colors occur due to the difference in energy among the valence shells of the s and p orbitals. Basically, this energy correlates to the wavelengths of visible light. Each alkali metal has a distinct color and can be recognised easily as lithium with crimson, sodium, potassium with golden yellow and rubidium, caesium with bluish violet color.

Day's Conclusion

On day 1, God created light and separated light from darkness. In period 1, there are only two elements—hydrogen and helium. Here, we see a separation between hydrogen and helium in the first period. They are mainly involved in the fusion reactions that generate light and heat. In the beginning of the universe, only light elements existed such as hydrogen and helium. Interactions between these two elements created the increasingly more complex elements and chemicals that built up the visible universe. These interactions originated from these fusion reactions in which light and heat were by-products. Group 1 alkali metals are known to react violently with cold water and release vast amounts of heat and light as well. Thus, again, period 1 and group 1 elements are highly associated with light, which also corresponds to day 1 creation.

Second Day of Creation and the Periodic Table

⁶Then God said, "Let there be a firmament in the midst of the waters, and let it divide the waters from the waters." ⁷Thus God made the firmament, and divided the waters which were under the firmament from the waters which were above the firmament; and it was so. ⁸And God called the firmament Heaven. So the evening and the morning were the second day. (Genesis 1:6–8, NKJV)

On the second day God made a firmament which separated the waters above from those below. The firmament is the sky conceived as a solid dome. The word *firmament* (*raqia* in Hebrew) is derived from *raqa*, the verb used in Hebrew for the act of beating metal into thin plates. In some translations, the firmament is not taken in the literal sense such as a solid dome or something metallic; instead, it is understood as a cover around the earth or the earth's atmospheric cover. In fact, it acts as a solid dome protecting Earth from tons of dust and sand-sized particles. As stated in Genesis, God created the firmament to separate the waters below the firmament from the waters above, just as the atmospheric pressure keeps liquid water on the surface of the earth. In the periodic tables second period and concurrent groups exhibit a parallel to the day's creation.

45

Periodic Table (Second Period and Second and Third Groups) and Second Day of Genesis

Group →

Period	IA	IIA	IIIB	IVB	VB	VIB	VIIB	VIII	VIII	VIII	IB	IIB	IIIA	IVA	VA	VIA	VIIA	0
1	1 H					SEPARATION BETWEEN WATERS												2 He
2	3 Li	4 Be											5 B	6 C	7 N	8 O	9 F	10 Ne
3	11 Na	12 Mg											13 Al	14 Si	15 P	16 S	17 Cl	18 Ar
4	19 K	20 Ca	21 Sc	22 Ti	23 V	24 Cr	25 Mn	26 Fe	27 Co	28 Ni	29 Cu	30 Zn	31 Ga	32 Ge	33 As	34 Se	35 Br	36 Kr
5	37 Rb	38 Sr	39 Y	40 Zr	41 Nb	42 Mo	43 Tc	44 Ru	45 Rh	46 Pd	47 Ag	48 Cd	49 In	50 Sn	51 Sb	52 Te	53 I	54 Xe
6	55 Cs	56 Ba	57 La	72 Hf	73 Ta	74 W	75 Re	76 Os	77 Ir	78 Pt	79 Au	80 Hg	81 Tl	82 Pb	83 Bi	84 Po	85 At	86 Rn
7	87 Fr	88 Ra	89 Ac	104 Rf	105 Db	106 Sg	107 Bh	108 Hs	109 Mt	110 Ds	111 Rg	112 Cn	113 Nh	114 Fl	115 Mc	116 Lv	117 Ts	118 Og

57 La	58 Ce	59 Pr	60 Nd	61 Pm	62 Sm	63 Eu	64 Gd	65 Tb	66 Dy	67 Ho	68 Er	69 Tm	70 Yb	71 Lu
89 Ac	90 Th	91 Pa	92 U	93 Np	94 Pu	95 Am	96 Cm	97 Bk	98 Cf	99 Es	100 Fm	101 Md	102 No	103 Lr

Second Day in Periods

The elements in the second period are lithium (Li), beryllium (Be), boron (B), carbon (C), nitrogen (N), oxygen (O), fluorine (F), and neon (Ne). In this period, we see a separation in the grid between beryllium (Be) and boron (B), representing the IIA and IIIA groups, respectively. The second period is the least metallic in comparison to the other periods with the exception of the first period, which cannot be compared because it contains only two elements. Lithium and beryllium are the only two metals in the period. Lithium (Li) is one of the three elements synthesized in the big bang,

46

making it a primordial element. Although it is widely distributed on Earth, it does not naturally occur in elemental form due to its high reactivity. The second element, beryllium (Be), is also a strong, hard, white-colored light rigid metal. The beryllium (Be) synthesized in stars is short-lived, and it is a relatively rare element in the universe. It is a bivalent element, found naturally only in combinations with other elements in minerals. After beryllium, there is a gap or separation in the period. The word *firmament* is used to define the act of beating metal into thin plates. Lithium is the first of the alkalis in the periodic table and is the lightest solid metal. It is soft, a silvery-white alkali metal. Beryllium is also a very soft and light metal. Therefore, both metals could be beaten due to their softness for making firmament as indicated in Genesis. There is a gap in the period after beryllium. The next element of IIIA group is boron. Boron is classified as a metalloid. It is produced entirely by cosmic ray spallation or fragmentation. Boron is concentrated on Earth by the water solubility of its compounds. It is volatile with steam. This may be the reason that boron is separated from beryllium and closer to the elements forming the atmosphere. It is concentrated on Earth due to the borate minerals. These are mined industrially as borax and kernite. These first three light elements, lithium, beryllium, and boron, are rare throughout the universe but areabundant among the primary galactic cosmic rays (GCRs). These cosmic rays come from outside the solar system but usually from within Milky Way galaxy. These cosmic rays are made up of atomic nucleus, which lost its electrons due to their high energy. Cosmic ray particles that arrive at the top of the Earth's atmosphere are termed primaries; their collisions with atmospheric nuclei like nitrogen give rise to secondaries.

Some theologians suggest that in the second day, a water canopy was created around the earth due to water separation. Today, we have ozone gases above the Earth's atmosphere. Perhaps, this ozone is a by-product of the interactions between the cosmic radiation and water of the water canopy. Now, it is interesting to note that during the Great Flood, the water rained down for forty days from this water canopy and filled the Earth. The raining canopy water contained these three elements with them. Furthermore, it is amazing to note how between Groups II A and III A, there are forty d-transitional elements, which symbolize the forty days of rain in the great flood.

As the cosmic radiation could not reach the Earth's surface due to this water canopy, lithium, beryllium, and boron were not present in the early Earth. Now, later on in the Bible, we read about the Great Flood, and we read that the people before the flood lived unusually long lives and were also extremely violent. According to G Schrauzer, there are numerous studies conducted in which many cities were studied throughout Texas. What was astonishing to find out from the water analysis is that those cities in which the water contained natural lithium, there was surprisingly low crime rate. We know now that lithium was not present during the early days of the Earth, and this may have been a reason as for extreme violence during those times. Boron increases neuron activities and cognitive performance, which may be leading factor to build a tower and the discovery of many new languages in Babel. Beryllium is listed as a carcinogen by the International Agency for Research on Cancer and responsible for shortening of human life span. According to Institute of Medicine, magnesium is needed in more than three hundred enzyme systems that regulate many biochemical reactions in the human body, like protein synthesis, muscle and nerve function, blood glucose control, and blood pressure regulation. And beryllium can replace magnesium easily in these enzymes, leading to malfunction of those enzymes, leading to shorter life span. As the flood caused the water canopy to extensively thin out leading to the arrival of the cosmic rays into Earth and with it, these three elements landed on the Earth that drastically cut down the violence and life span but increased the cognitive function.

After boron, every element participates in the formation of the atmosphere. Carbon (C) is the sixth most abundant element in the universe and plays an important role in the chemistry of life. In molecular form, carbon is found as carbon dioxide (CO_2) in the atmosphere of the Earth and found in all natural waters. Coal, petroleum, and natural gas are chiefly hydrocarbons. Carbon is unique among the elements in the vast number and variety of compounds it can form. It is found free in nature in three allotropic forms: amorphous, graphite, and diamond. The most important compound of carbon in the Earth's atmosphere are carbon dioxide, carbon monoxide, methane, and black carbon. Nitrogen is an odorless, tasteless, colorless, nonmetallic chemical element that appears in great abundance in the Earth's atmosphere. It is the seventh most abundant element in the universe. Nitrogen constitutes 78 percent of Earth's atmosphere and is a constituent of all living cells. Nitrogen is an essential element for life because it is an essential ingredient of DNA. Nitrogen molecules occur mainly in air but can be found in water and soils, in the form of nitrates and nitrites. Oxygen is the third most abundant element in the universe and is the most abundant chemical element by mass in the Earth's biosphere, air, sea, and land. Oxygen is colorless, odorless, and tasteless gas. Oxygen constitutes 21 percent of Earth's atmosphere and is a constituent of all living tissues.

Fluorine is a highly reactive nonmetal with atomic symbol F. It is a yellow-green gas that is not found in a free state. It is the lightest halogen and occurs as a highly toxic

49

diatomic gas at standard conditions. Fluorine is the thirteenth most common element in the crust of Earth. s.

Neon is a colorless, odorless gas. It is nearly inert toward all elements and chemicals. Neon is rare on Earth, but is abundant on a universal scale; it is the fifth most abundant element in the universe by mass, after hydrogen, helium, oxygen, and carbon. Neon is monatomic, making it lighter than the molecules of diatomic nitrogen and oxygen that form the bulk of Earth's atmosphere. It is a very interesting link that carbon, nitrogen, and oxygen are the main contents of the atmosphere.

So the second day of creation and the second period of the elements connect to each other with formation of atmosphere separating waters of below from that of above.

Moreover, there is a gap between beryllium and boron in the second period indicating the separation.

Second Day in Groups

Group IIA is composed of beryllium (Be), magnesium (Mg), calcium (Ca), strontium (Sr), barium (Ba), and radium (Ra). Group IIA elements are known as alkaline earth metals. The Group IIA elements are all metals with a shiny, silvery-white color. The Group II metals become more reactive toward the water as we go down the Group. Group IIIA contains boron (B), aluminium (Al), gallium (Ga), indium (In), thallium (Tl), and Nihonium (Nh). These elements have also been called as earth metals.

It is remarkable that the gap between the columns of the IIA and IIIA groups is found only between beryllium and boron as well as between magnesium and aluminium, respectively, in the IIA and IIIA elements. These four elements, Be, Mg, B, and Al, do not react directly with water. However, it is chemically proven that the remaining alkaline earth metals (IIA Group) and earth metals (IIIA Group) react with water. These alkaline earth metals directly react with water to form strongly alkaline hydroxides and should be handled carefully. It has been observed that the heavier metals react more vigorously compared to the lighter alkaline earth metals. Beryllium does not react with water. Magnesium does not appear to react with water because an outer layer of solid magnesium oxide (MgO) forms and protects the rest of the metal. Calcium reacts with water instantly. Thus we see a water separation between magnesium and calcium in the second group. Calcium is a white and relatively soft metal. It reacts vigorously with water to produce hydrogen gas and a cloudy white precipitate of calcium hydroxide.

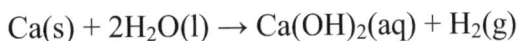

$$Ca(s) + 2H_2O(l) \rightarrow Ca(OH)_2(aq) + H_2(g)$$

Strontium reacts with water to produce strontium hydroxide and hydrogen gas. In comparison to calcium, strontium reacts faster with water.

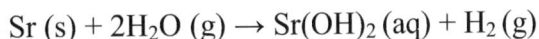

$$Sr\ (s) + 2H_2O\ (g) \rightarrow Sr(OH)_2\ (aq) + H_2\ (g)$$

Barium reacts readily with water to form barium hydroxide, $Ba(OH)_2$, and hydrogen gas (H_2). The reaction is quicker than that of strontium.

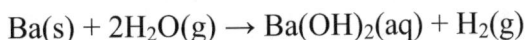

$$Ba(s) + 2H_2O(g) \rightarrow Ba(OH)_2(aq) + H_2(g)$$

Radium probably reacts very readily with water to form radium hydroxide, $Ra(OH)_2$ and hydrogen gas (H_2). The reaction is expected to be quicker than that of barium.

$$Ra(s) + 2H_2O(g) \rightarrow Ra(OH)_2(aq) + H_2(g)$$

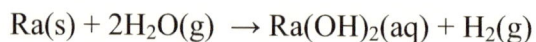

In IIIA elements, boron is the only element that is not a metal, behaving like a metalloid. Aluminium is the third most abundant element in the earth's crust, being slightly less reactive than the active metals. The other three elements in this group are active metals but are so scarce that they are of limited interestIn fact, boron (B) does not react at with water. One notable reaction within this group is aluminium's (Al) reaction with water. Aluminium does not appear to react with water because an outer layer of solid aluminium oxide (Al_2O_3) forms and protects the rest of the metal. Due to the low melting point, gallium dissolves in water. Thus, we see a water separation between aluminium and gallium in the third group.

These four elements, Be and Mg of Group IIA and Boron and Aluminium of Group IIIA, do not react directly with water, so they are separated from other elements of the respective groups as they dissolve in water instantly. This separation by water shows a direct correlation with the second day of creation told in Genesis.

Day's Conclusion

On Day 2, God did not particularly create anything. Verses 6–8 suggest that on Day 2, God only separated the skies from the water. Correspondingly, we see a big energy gap between the first and second orbitals. When considering periods, day 2 correlates with period 2 as our atmosphere is mainly made up of nitrogen and oxygen present in the second period. Within period 2, there is a separation or gap between beryllium and boron. The elements within a period

52

do not share any particular characteristic or pattern—they only share in the fact that they are on the same energy level. In terms of group, day 2 parallels not just with Group IIA but also with IIIA to represent the two ends of the separation present within the periodic table. Within group IIA and group IIIA, the four elements—beryllium, magnesium, magnesium, and aluminium—do not react with water while the rest of the elements in both groups form hydroxides. So, the elements of both period 2, as well as groups II A and III A closely parallel the "event" of Day 2.

Third Day of Creation and the Periodic Table

⁹Then God said, "Let the waters under the heavens be gathered together into one place, and let the dry land appear"; and it was so. ¹⁰And God called the dry land Earth, and the gathering together of the waters He called Seas. And God saw that it was good. ¹¹Then God said, "Let the earth bring forth grass, the herb that yields seed, and the fruit tree that yields fruit according to its kind, whose seed is in itself, on the earth"; and it was so. ¹²And the earth brought forth grass, the herb that yields seed according to its kind, and the tree that yields fruit, whose seed is in itself according to its kind. And God saw that it was good. ¹³So the evening and the morning were the third day. (Genesis 1:9–13, NKJV)

On day third, God separated water from the land, calling them earth and sea. It's interesting that in the first three days of creation, we see different kinds of separation. First, light and darkness; on the second day, water from water; and on the third day, water separates from land creating dry land for vegetation. According to Genesis, God commanded that the dry land be vegetative and the first plants appear on land. In the periodic table, we also find a similar separation or gap in the first three periods with the elements in these periods possessing the properties that

54

correlate to the days of creation described in Genesis. In the third period, surprisingly, there is also a separation and the elements possess the properties required for biological life.

Periodic Table (Third Period and Fourth Group) and Third Day of Genesis

Periodic Table

Third Day in Period

The elements in the third period are sodium (Na), magnesium (Mg), aluminum (Al), silicon (Si), phosphorus (P), sulfur (S), chlorine (Cl), and argon (Ar). One of the first things to note is that there is a separation between IIA element, magnesium, and IIIA element, aluminum.

Furthermore, on the third day, recall God separated the dry land from the waters and created vegetation. Now, the

56

elements that correlate to Day 3 are silicon, magnesium, phosphorus, and sulfur.

Sodium

Third day starts with seawater, and we know that seawater is saline because it contains sodium chloride. Sodium and chlorine are the predominant elements of sea and found in the third period of the periodic table. Moreover, sodium is considered beneficial element because it promotes growth in many plant species.

Magnesium

Third day witnessed the eruption of the crust of Earth. Magnesium is found along with iron in the mantle of Earth just below the crust of Earth. Bible clearly separates the continental crust from mantle of Earth, which is confirmed by the gap between magnesium and aluminum in the third period.

Aluminum

On the third day, Earth's crust abruptly appeared from sea. Aluminum is the third most abundant element of Earth's crust after oxygen and silicon in the form of aluminum silicates.

Silicon

More than 90% of the Earth's crust is made of silicate minerals. This has made silicon the second most abundant element after oxygen. Even more interesting is the fact that sand is found on at the seashores (dry land separated from the waters). The composition of sand varies depending on local rocks and environmental conditions. However, the main component of sand in inland continental as well as nontropical coastal settings is silica (SiO_2).

Magnesium

Now, on to magnesium in plant life. Magnesium is vital for the survival of plants, a.k.a. vegetation. This element plays a crucial role in photosynthesis. In the compound chlorophyll, a magnesium ion is at the center surrounded by four nitrogen atoms as shown below.

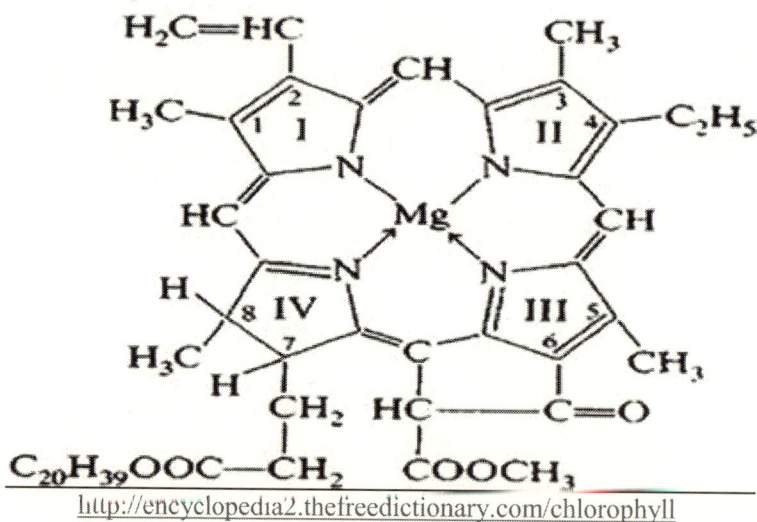

Magnesium assists the chlorophyll molecule to capture sunlight, which, in turn, keeps the electrons in an excited state for transferring them to other molecules to create sugar.

58

Phosphorus

Phosphorus is crucial as it is one of the fundamental constituents of amino acids, proteins, nucleic acids, and most importantly, DNA. During the first two days, DNA or the genetic code was not really necessary; however, during the third day, vegetation—DNA is necessary for vegetation to propagate. The mention of seed in Genesis suggests the propagation or procreation of vegetation, which would require DNA or the blueprint of life. As we can see in the following diagram, phosphorus combines with sugar to form the backbone of DNA.

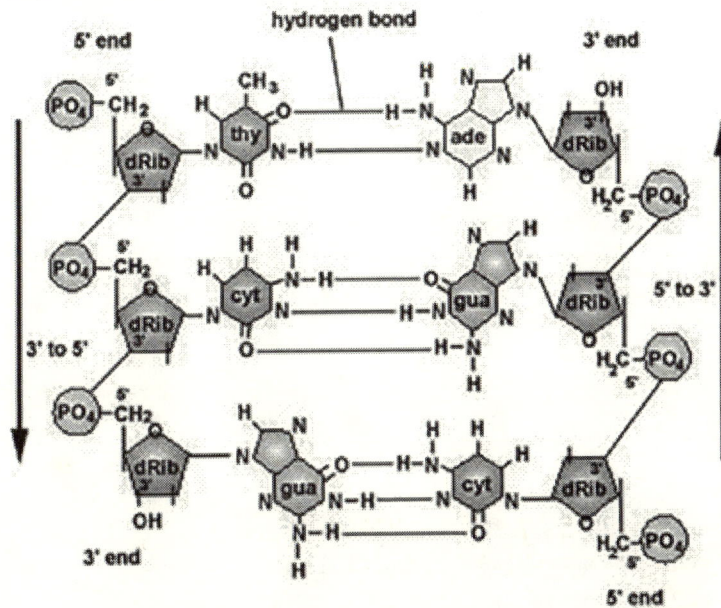

http://faculty.ccbcmd.edu/biotutorials/dna/fg16.html

The nucleic acids, in particular DNA, represent the blueprint of life. DNA codes for genes, which when transcribed leads to a RNA transcript, which is then

59

translated into amino acids, which form proteins. Proteins are molecules that serve a variety of functions in the cells of organisms to keep them functioning and alive. Phosphorus is also found in adenosine triphosphate, or ATP, the molecule that stores and releases energy for cellular function.

Sulfur

Sulfur is needed for nitrogen fixation in plants. Nitrogen fixation is a vital process of plant life in which nitrogen is absorbed from the atmosphere and used in the composition of organic compounds and ammonia. Furthermore, sulfur and its various compounds are considered as a natural defence for plants. People who grow plants know that sulfur is used as a fungicide as well as help in the management of plant disease. Sulfur compounds also play numerous roles in the synthesis and function of chlorophyll in plants. Thus, sulfur, found in the third period, is vital for the creation of the third day—vegetation or plant life.

Chlorine

Chlorine is considered an essential element because it is required for plant metabolism and the completion of the life cycle of the plants. Chlorine also plays important role in photosynthesis as chlorine is needed in the water splitting system. Chlorine is vital for the opening and closing of stomata in plant leaves. Chlorine is also needed for the synthesis of chloroplast.

Third Day in Group

As mentioned previously, Group IIIA correlates with the second day of creation. Therefore, Group IVA correlates with the third day of creation. This group is also known as the carbon family and consists of carbon (C), silicon (Si), germanium (Ge), tin (Sn), lead (Pb), and flerovium (Fl).

Carbon

As we know, in the third day of creation, living organisms are first created—vegetation is indeed considered as living organism. Carbon is important as it is the backbone of all cellular, living organisms. Everything that makes up cells and other structures in living organisms are known as organic compounds—organic typically refers to the presence of carbon in these compounds. Carbon is vital to life as it is a stable element that can form millions of compounds with other carbon atoms and other elements that can be arranged in a myriad of ways. This allows for the production of stable, as well as diverse compounds that are necessary for the functions of life. Mostly everything within every living organism, with the exception of water, is made up of carbon.

Carbon also has a major role in photosynthesis. Plants use energy from the sun and chlorophyll molecules to turn gaseous carbon dioxide from the atmosphere into glucose, a process called carbon fixation.

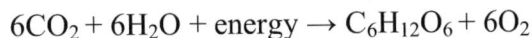

$$6CO_2 + 6H_2O + energy \rightarrow C_6H_{12}O_6 + 6O_2$$

In aerobic respiration, plants break down glucose into carbon dioxide and water (as shown in the equation below) and use this energy to fuel biological activities.

$$C_6H_{12}O_6 + 6O_2 \rightarrow 6CO_2 + 6H_2O + energy$$

Silicon

Silicon is the second most abundant element in the Earth's crust as well as the most abundant, if not a significant component of most soil. By mass, 15 percent of silicon is found in the Earth's composition along with the other elements. The Earth's interior is made up of layers of various elements, including silicon as well. The crust is composed of relatively low-dense silicates. The mantle, on the other hand, has higher and dense iron-rich silicates. The core also has silicon mixed with iron compounds as the makeup of the core. So the third day, that separation of water and land, is parallel with the elements in Group IV.

Furthermore, silicon possesses astoundingly similar chemical properties to that of carbon. Silicon has the ability to create molecules that can convey biological information, like carbon—this is the only element other than carbon that is stable and versatile to do so. Silicon is also found in the cell wall of primitive living systems like sponges and diatoms, a type of algae. Moreover, silicon is considered a beneficial element because it promotes growth in many plant species.

Now mushrooms are not plants but have seeds and grow in ground. The mushrooms also need carbon, sulphur, phosphorus, and magnesium for their growth and development.

Days Conclusion

We read how God separated dry ground or land from water or seas. This is therefore another separation and the final separation in creation process. We see a parallel separation in the third period between Group IIA element magnesium and Group IIIA element aluminum. Furthermore, God created vegetation or plant life. The key elements within Period 3 as well as Group IVA correlate to the separation of land and water. This includes the presence of silicon in the sand or sea shores as well as in the Earth's interior and soils. Furthermore, carbon, magnesium, and phosphorus are key elements for the living organisms, including plants.

Fourth Day of Creation and the Periodic Table

¹⁴Then God said, "Let there be lights in the firmament of the heavens to divide the day from the night; and let them be for signs and seasons, and for days and years; ¹⁵and let them be for lights in the firmament of the heavens to give light on the earth"; and it was so.
¹⁶Then God made two great lights: the greater light to rule the day, and the lesser light to rule the night. He made the stars also. ¹⁷God set them in the firmament of the heavens to give light on the earth, ¹⁸and to rule over the day and over the night, and to divide the light from the darkness. And God saw that it was good. ¹⁹So the evening and the morning were the fourth day. (Genesis 1:14–19, NKJV)

Now, we read that on the fourth day, the sun, the moon, and the stars are brought into existence. Now this would appear to be a contradiction—sunlight is essential for the existence of life and thus vegetation as well (photosynthesis is the process of gaining energy from sunlight), and we know vegetation was brought about on the third day. So it must mean that living systems started without sunlight deep down in the earth and oceans. For examples, *Shewanella* and *Geobacter*, two kinds of bacteria, consume electrons directly from their surroundings as their sources of energy to survive. *Desulforudis audaxviator*, another bacterium,

64

does not need organic compounds, light, or oxygen to live. We also know that *Methylococcaceae* and *Methylocystaceae* can use methane as their source of energy. Now it is interesting to note that *Methylomirabilis oxyfera* uses methane and nitrogen oxide to make its own internal oxygen. This all indicates that there was a time in the Earth when living systems do not need sunlight or oxygen for survival.

However, we know that on the first day, God created the heavens, the earth, and light—this must mean that the stars were present from the first day itself. I believe that hence, the fourth day of creation symbolizes the new generation of stars. In astronomy, we learn that there are three classes or generations of stars. The older generation of stars had a significantly shorter life span and were not able to host rocky or terrestrial planets such as the Earth. This is in comparison to our sun, which is a new generation yellow dwarf or main sequence star. A comparison of the day with the periodic table also shows this amazing correlation with elements that determine new heavenly bodies from old.

Periodic Table (Fourth Period and Fifth Group) and Fourth Day of Genesis

Fourth Day in Period

In the periodic table's fourth period, there are eighteen elements. The main elements are potassium (K), calcium (Ca), gallium (Ga), germanium (Ge), arsenic (As), selenium (Se), bromine (Br), and krypton (Kr). The remaining ten transition elements are scandium (Sc), titanium (Ti), vanadium (V), chromium (Cr), manganese (Mn), iron (Fe), cobalt (Co), nickel (Ni), copper (Cu), and zinc (Zn).

The major element of concern that correlates with the fourth day of creation is iron (Fe). Iron is not only the most common element in the sun and stars, it is also the largest

66

element that can be produced in supergiant stars. In a way, one can consider iron to be the most desired element of the universe because iron[56] has the lowest energy density of any isotope of any element. Due to this factor, cooling process in stars ends at iron. Supergiant stars can fuse elements up to iron in the cooling process before they either collapse into white dwarfs or explode in supernovae explosions making elements higher than iron.

Stars are classified by their chemical composition called metallicity, which describes the chemical composition of elements beyond hydrogen and helium. Metallicity is often expressed as a ratio "[Fe/H]", the logarithm of the ratio of a star's iron abundance compared to that of the hydrogen content. Based on this understanding, metallicity also indicates the age of an astronomical object. Older stars (from the early universe) have lower metallicity in comparison to newer stars. This means that older stars don't have much iron in their composition.

This all leads to stellar population, a term that refers to a single generation of stars characterized by a common age and chemical composition. There are three stellar populations, (I, II, III), with each group having decreasing metal content and increasing age. So Population III stars are near pristine stars as they are made of only hydrogen and helium, along with a very small amount of lithium. They are also the oldest stars. Population II stars have more metal content than Population III stars, but not as much as Population I stars. Our sun, on the other hand, is a high metal Population I star. So as can be seen, this all points to a new star creation on the fourth day.

Also, the moon is specifically and only mentioned on the fourth day of creation whereas we know that "the heavens and the earth" were mentioned from the very first day. Astronomers agree that our moon formed much later than the development of the Solar System, which is in agreement with the biblical account of the creation of the heavenly bodies. Furthermore, the surface of the moon predominantly contains many of the fourth period elements such as potassium, calcium, titanium, manganese, chromium, and iron—again, revealing how the periodic table clearly describes the creation account.

Moreover, the fourth period (n=4) starts with potassium, in which the added electrons go to the 4s orbital. Here it is notable to mention that before the 4p orbital is full, the 3d orbitals (in the transition elements) are filled as that is more energetically favorable. The first d orbitals are introduced in this period. Starting with scandium (Z=21) with the electronic configuration of $3d^1 4s^2$, the 3d orbitals are filled one element at a time, till zinc (Z=30) with electronic configuration of $3d^{10}4s^2$. The fourth period ends with krypton and a complete 4p orbital. So this period introduces a new energy level with the beginning of d orbitals and transition elements. Similarly, on the fourth day of creation, God introduced a new energy source into the universe with the creation of new stars such as the sun and other Population I stars, which laid the foundation for life as we currently know it.

The fourth day of creation is linked to Group VA. This group is known as the nitrogen family and consists of nitrogen (N), phosphorus (P), arsenic (As), antimony (Sb), bismuth (Bi), and moscovium (Mc) In this group, nitrogen, phosphorus, and arsenic, in particular, correlate perfectly with the fourth day of creation. Numerous astronomical studies indicate the presence of these three elements in the sun, moon, stars, and meteorites. As we see, the fourth day indicates a new source of energy, which is confirmed in this group as newer and bigger stars use a new way to produce nuclear energy using nitrogen.

Nitrogen

Nitrogen plays a leading role in larger stars to create energy. The Carbon-Nitrogen-Oxygen (CNO) cycle is a cyclic catalytic process or nuclear reaction in which nitrogen fuses with hydrogen ion (proton) and makes helium, releasing heat and light. In this cyclic reaction, carbon, nitrogen, and oxygen are the by-products. Only hydrogen is converted into helium to produce the energy. In this cycle four, hydrogen atoms are used to make one helium along with energy. Below is the equation for the CNO cycle.

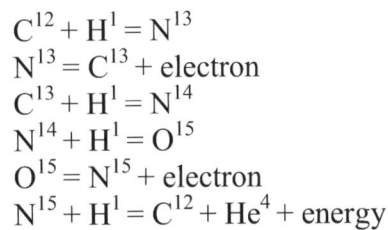

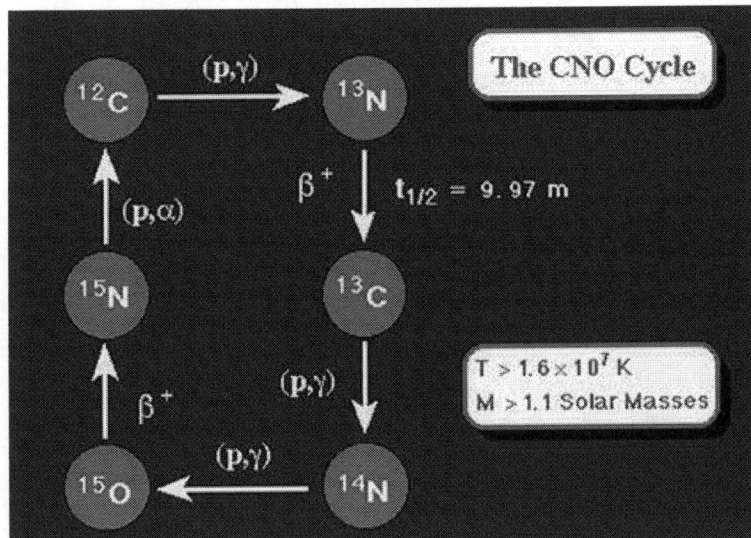

$$C^{12} + H^1 = N^{13}$$
$$N^{13} = C^{13} + electron$$
$$C^{13} + H^1 = N^{14}$$
$$N^{14} + H^1 = O^{15}$$
$$O^{15} = N^{15} + electron$$
$$N^{15} + H^1 = C^{12} + He^4 + energy$$

69

http://csep10.phys.utk.edu/astr162/lect/energy/cno.html

What's more is that astronomers are analyzing the light that we detect from stars to determine numerous aspects of the stars such as the chemical features, the element's derivation, the star's age, as well as the development of galaxies and universe. Currently, astronomers have detected the presence of arsenic and selenium in ancient stars located in the faint stellar halo that surrounds our galaxy, the Milky Way. Thus, the elements within Group 5 correlate to the creation of the heavenly bodies as recorded in the Scriptures.

Phosphorus

The term *phosphorus* comes from a Greek word meaning "bearer of light," and it delivers on that promise. The two common forms of phosphorus are white phosphorus, and red phosphorus. White phosphorus gives off a slight glow in air and self-ignites in room air at 30^0C so it is used in fireworks. Red phosphorus is used in safety matchboxes.

Day's Conclusion

In verses 14–19, God created the sun, moon, and stars on the fourth day. As we saw, the elements within period 4 such as iron, as well as the elements within Group 5 such as nitrogen relate to the creation of day 4. These elements are strongly present in the heavenly bodies as well as point to a new generation of stars, that which replaced the old generation of stars that were present in the beginning. The biblical account of creation in so little words carries significant depth and detail that we are only beginning to unravel with our advances in knowledge.

Fifth Day of Creation and the Periodic Table

[20]Then God said, "Let the waters abound with an abundance of living creatures, and let birds fly above the earth across the face of the firmament of the heavens." [21]So God created great sea creatures and every living thing that moves, with which the waters abounded, according to their kind, and every winged bird according to its kind. And God saw that it was good. [22]And God blessed them, saying, "Be fruitful and multiply, and fill the waters in the seas, and let birds multiply on the earth." [23]So the evening and the morning were the fifth day. (Genesis 1:20–23, NKJV)

God created sea creatures and birds, thus, the fifth day of creation marks the arrival of animal kingdom on the face of the earth. As we know, every organism is dependent on different elements for their sustained growth and development. At every stage, few elements in the primitive earth played a major role in the making up of different life-forms. The comparison of the day to the periodic table exactly strikes out two key elements Molybdenum (Mo) and Iodine (I) in the fifth period and the subsequent group, respectively, which gave a threshold in developing complex life-forms which were mobile organisms. Thus, like all previous days of creation, the fifth day of creation parallels

72

the characteristics of the elements in accordance with the day of creation.

Periodic Table (Fifth Period and Sixth Group) and Fifth Day of Genesis

Fifth Day in Period

The fifth period contains eighteen elements: rubidium, strontium, yttrium, zirconium, niobium, molybdenum, technetium, ruthenium, rhodium, palladium, silver, cadmium, indium, tin, antimony, tellurium, iodine, and xenon.

Numerous studies show that most of the elements in fifth period are used by one or another marine creature. For example, octopus need Rb, Sr, and Cd. Seabirds use Rb, Mo, and Cd. Marine planktons use Sr, Ag, Sn, and Sb. Sea cucumbers use Zr and Nb. Many molluscs, crustaceans, and fishes use Rh, Pd, In, and Te. Ru is used by marine algae and sea bottom fish named Pleuronects. Squids named *Ommastrephes* uses Cd. *Artemia salina* uses Y. The comparison of the day to the periodic table exactly strikes out two key elements, molybdenum (Mo) and Iodine(I). Molybdenum is essential for the biological assimilation of nitrogen and iodine (I) controls metabolism. Thus, like all previous days of creation, the fifth day of creation parallels the characteristics of the elements in accordance with the day of creation.

Fifth Day in Group

The fifth day of creation is linked to Group VIA, known as the oxygen family. It contains oxygen (O), sulfur (S), selenium (Se), tellurium (Te), polonium (Po), and livermorium (Lv). The animal kingdom depends on oxygen to flourish. From fish to birds, they thrive on oxygen for respiration and metabolism. Isotopic studies of different period sediment indicate that at some point of time, the Earth's atmosphere and oceans were anoxic (without oxygen). Mass-independent fractionalization of sulfur isotopes could only form in the absence of oxygen. Later molecular oxygen came forth due to the action of photosynthetic cyanobacteria in much lower amounts compared to its present atmospheric level. A more oxygen-rich ocean created ideal conditions for animals to survive because they have a higher requirement for oxygen. These included the first predatory animals, marking the beginning

74

of a modern marine biosphere with the type of food webs we are familiar with today.

In the fifth day, we see fishes and birds together. There are some similarities as to how birds and fishes deal with the oxygen.

In fish, heart pumps blood to the gills where gas exchange occurs. The oxygenated blood then passes on to the capillary networks that supply oxygen to the rest of the body. Then the deoxygenated blood returns to the atrium. This is a unidirectional flow of oxygen.

In birds, the respiratory cycle involves two inspirations and two expirations. Birds have three sets of lungs, anterior (cranial) air sacs, posterior (caudal) air sacs, and the lungs themselves. Air is shifted around these three sets of respiratory organs during inhalation and exhalation with the mechanism as described below:

1. During the first inspiration, the air stream travels to the caudal (posterior) air sacs. During the first expiration, the air is moved from the posterior air sacs into the lungs. Blood capillaries flow through the lungs, and the oxygen and carbon dioxide are exchanged.
2. When the bird inspires the second time, the air moves to the cranial air sacs. On the second expiration, the air moves out of the cranial air sacs, into the trachea, and out of the nostrils. This is also a unidirectional flow of oxygen.

Air sacs permit a unidirectional flow of air through the lungs. Unidirectional flow means that the air moving through the bird's lungs is largely fresh air with higher oxygen content. By contrast, air flow is bidirectional in mammals, moving back and forth into and out of the lungs.

As a result, air coming into a mammal's lungs is mixed with *old* air (air that has been in the lungs for a while), and this mixed air has less oxygen. So, in the bird's lungs, more oxygen is available to diffuse into the blood. In other words, birds and fishes have a flow-through respiratory system with interconnecting tubes for continuous flow rather than blindended alveoli in human lungs where gases become mixed.

Another commonality between birds and fishes is that they have nucleated red blood cells whereas mammals have nonnucleated red blood cell. The red blood cells contain a pigment called hemoglobin. The primary function of hemoglobin is to transport oxygen. Since oxygen is not very soluble in water, hemoglobin is the oxygen transport protein used in the blood of fish and birds. A hemoglobin molecule is composed of four polypeptide chains as a cross. Each chain contains one heme group containing one iron ion. This iron is the site of oxygen binding. Each iron ion can bind one O_2 molecule thus each hemoglobin molecule is capable of binding four O_2 molecules.

Sulfur is the second element of group VIA which also has similarly important roles in the lives of both sea animals and birds. Sulfur is one of the components that make up proteins and vitamins. Sulfur is important for the functioning of proteins and enzymes in plants and animals. Generally, it is found in many essential compounds like cysteine and methionine amino acids, with some oxidation products and certain reserve or osmoprotectant molecules such as S-methyl methionine and various types of sulfonates. Many derivatives of sulfur take part in secondary metabolism where these sulfur-containing metabolites like sulfated carbohydrates and aminoglycosides play an efficient role in the immune system.

Selenium

Selenium is used by diatoms, sea urchin, and many marine fishes. Selenium is also found in thyroid of many marine fishes.

Tellurium

Tellurium is used by bacteria and deep ocean hydrothermal vent worms and tubeworms for respiration.

Days Conclusion

On the fifth day, God created the animals of the air and of those under the water. In period 5, two key elements, molybdenum and iodine, play key roles in the metabolism of both fishes and birds. In group 6, the key element to consider is oxygen. Living organisms and, in particular, animal life require oxygen for respiration. Furthermore, both fish and birds have nucleated red blood cells, which carry oxygen, the key element from group 6. It is remarkable how closely the elements given in the periodic table correlate with the account of creation.

Sixth Day of Creation and the Periodic Table

[24]Then God said, "Let the earth bring forth the living creature according to its kind: cattle and creeping thing and beast of the earth, each according to its kind"; and it was so. [25]And God made the beast of the earth according to its kind, cattle according to its kind, and everything that creeps on the earth according to its kind. And God saw that it was good.

[26]Then God said, "Let Us make man in Our image, according to Our likeness; let them have dominion over the fish of the sea, over the birds of the air, and over the cattle, over all[b] the earth and over every creeping thing that creeps on the earth."

[27]So God created man in His own image; in the image of God He created him; male and female He created them. [28]Then God blessed them, and God said to them, "Be fruitful and multiply; fill the earth and subdue it; have dominion over the fish of the sea, over the birds of the air, and over every living thing that moves on the earth."

[29]And God said, "See, I have given you every herb that yields seed which is on the face of all the earth, and every tree whose fruit yields seed; to you it shall be for food. [30]Also, to every beast of the earth, to every bird of the air, and to everything that creeps on the earth, in which

there is life, I have given every green herb for food"; and it was so. [31]Then God saw everything that He had made, and indeed it was very good. So the evening and the morning were the sixth day. (Genesis 1:24–31, NKJV)

On the sixth day, God created all living creatures according to their kinds, which move on the ground. This included all of the wild beasts, livestock, reptiles, etc., in pairs. According to Genesis, God then created His most precious of all creations: man. Human beings are dearest to God in all of His creations as it is mentioned; God created human beings in His own "image" and "likeness" as male and female and gave them the authority over the fishes, birds, cattle, wild animals, and all types of creatures that live in sea, skies, and land. Humans are the representative or counterpart of God on the earth and are the only one to enter into a relationship with God spiritually. Scientifically, it is proven that *Homo sapiens* is the brainiest animal. The tendency to seek and self-analyze are the major differences between humans and other animals. The inner qualities of being mentally rational and alongside social and moral in nature set humans apart from the animal world. Physiological differences between humans and other animals are so low that there is no ready explanation as to why superiority was only attained by man. Unique human qualities and traits set man apart from the animals either by class or in degree. Thus, it can be easily said that because of our inner traits, man dominates the world. Only humans possess spiritual features that no other animal demonstrates. Everything we are because of everything we possess within ourselves. This day presents the most precious of all creations of God in the form of human beings on earth as men and women in the image of God. Being in the image of God is an immaterial possession, a mysterious gift to mankind, which enables him to dominate the world. Man in the Bible is described as the salt and the light of the earth (Matthew 5:13–16), meaning something of great worth and reliability. It is interesting to find that the periodic table's sixth period and subsequent group symbolizes the sixth day as the elements in the period and group represent Godly image is an inner image and values of material life as a social being.

Periodic Table (Sixth Period and Seventh Group) and Sixth Day of Genesis

Sixth Day in Period

In the sixth period, there are eighteen elements: caesium

(Cs), barium (Ba), lanthanum (La), hafnium (Hf), tantalum (Ta), tungsten (W), rhenium (Re), osmium (Os), iridium (Ir), platinum (Pt), gold (Au), mercury (Hg), thallium (Tl), lead (Pb), bismuth (Bi), polonium (Po), astatine (At), and radon (Rn). With the exception of these elements, fourteen elements of lanthanides are also considered in the sixth period, including cerium (Ce), praseodymium (Pr), neodymium (Nd), promethium (Pm), samarium (Sm), europium (Eu), gadolinium (Gd), terbium (Tb), dysprosium (Dy), holmium (Ho), erbium (Er), thulium (Tm), ytterbium (Yb), and lutetium (Lu).

Out of all of these, the lanthanide series had special characteristics that are associated with the sixth day of creation. This series consists of the fourteen elements, (atomic numbers 58 to 71), and that follow lanthanum on the periodic table have an oxidation state of +3 like lanthnum. These fourteen, along with the actinides (atomic numbers 90 through 103), are set aside from the periodic table as f block elements. Actinides, which are also f block elements, do not share characteristics like lanthanides. For example, thorium has +4 oxidation state, protactinium has +5 oxidation state, uranium has +6 oxidation state, and neptunium has +7 oxidation state. Thus, actinides do not show chemical similarity with actinium but to other transition metals. The best way to understanding the lanthanide series is by imagining nesting dolls (a set of wooden dolls of decreasing size placed one inside the other). It is very similar to the elements in the lanthanides series, which emerge from the previous elements. This happens because, in the sixth period, elements with four types of electron-filling shells are found: s-block, f-block, d-block, and p-block. Lanthanides and actinides are the only elements that fill the f-orbital. The complex electronic structure of the lanthanides is largely a mystery. The filling up of the f-shell is not readily explained in the theoretical treatment of atoms and molecules with the result that we are still struggling to understand these elements at the bottom of the periodic table. In theory, the bonding orbitals in the lanthanide series should be 4f, 5d, and 6s. Traditionally, it has been viewed as the contracted f-shell orbitals are shielded. Lanthanides are image elements of lanthanum. Lanthanides are chemically similar to lanthanum as electrons go into inner f orbitals so the outer electronic structure of lanthanides remains similar to lanthanum. There is a decrease in the radii of lanthanide atoms as they increase in atomic number, in other words, the higher the atomic number, the smaller the radius. This decrease is known as the lanthanide contraction and aids in the process of separation by ion exchange. Lanthanide contraction reminds us that we cannot become greater than God. As all of the elements in the series have similar physical properties, the same +3 oxidation states, and similar chemical reactions with water, oxygen, and halogens, thus they are image elements of lanthanum. It is more astonishing to know that actinides also have similar atomic structure like lanthanides but actinides have multiple oxidation states and do not resemble actinium. It is amazing to find that the lanthanide series in the sixth period starts at the third group which enables them to be image elements, symbolic of the human inner nature which is considered to be an image of the Trinity God.

Sixth Day in Group

Group VIIA is the subsequent group that which correlates to the sixth day of creation. There are six elements in the group,

82

known as the halogen family or chlorine family, containing fluorine (F), chlorine (Cl), bromine (Br), iodine (I), astatine (At), and tennessine (Ts). Halogen is a Greek word meaning "salt maker" as the four elements of this group are involved in salt formation. It represents human beings biblically as man is said to be the salt of the earth (Matthew 5:13–16) and is a way of describing the importance of mankind. When we study the chemistry of all of the halogen elements, only four elements are taken into account as other elements like astatine and tennessine are radioactive and artificially made with a short life span. Halogens are reactive in nature and have seven electrons in their outer shells, giving them an oxidation number of -1. They bond covalently with another atom of the same element in order to gain an extra electron and achieve a full octet, forming diatomic molecules in their pure forms. Again, this correlates to the sixth day of creation where God created all higher animals, including Man, as male and female pairs, similar to how halogens form diatomic molecules. Fluorine, in the form of fluoride, is a micronutrient for human. It increases tooth resistance to decay and to prevent dental cavities, and to stimulate healthy bone growth. Chlorine, in the form of chloride, is an essential mineral for humans. It is needed for fluid and acid-base balance. Bromine as bromide is essential for tissue development in humans and all other animals, as the unique and essential role for ionic bromide as a co-factor, says a team of researchers led by Prof Billy Hudson of Vanderbilt University School of Medicine. The group VIIA element iodine plays an important role in numerous essential biological processes to maintain metabolism in the animal kingdom, and it plays a critical role in the development and functioning of the human brain. Thus, the elements of the group also correlate with the sixth day of creation.

Days Conclusion

In verses 24–31, God created land animals and man. Man is created in the image of God. Likewise, the Period 6 element lanthanum has fourteen image elements and parallels the godly image by which man is created. Furthermore, it is very interesting to note the link between Revelation 4:5, which states that God has seven spirits, and the seven f orbital, which is characteristic of the lanthanides. As the f orbital is an inner orbital, the godly image is an inner experience not outer appearance. Now, the Group VIIA elements, the halogens, are diatomic molecules that have nonpolar, covalent, single bonds. It is interesting to note that "so God created man in his own image, in the image of God he created him; male and female he created them" (Genesis 1:27). There is a close parallel, especially in the creation of man and woman, as well as their inner lives, to sixth-day creation that strongly relates to the elements of the corresponding groups and periods. Genesis 2:8 And the Lord God planted a garden eastward in Eden; and there he put the man whom he had formed. Again, we can see that halogen which represents the sixth day of creation is found in the east side of the periodic table.

Seventh Day of Creation and the Periodic Table

> Thus the heavens and the earth, and all the host of them, were finished. [2]And on the seventh day God ended His work which He had done, and He rested on the seventh day from all His work which He had done. [3]Then God blessed the seventh day and sanctified it, because in it He rested from all His work which God had created and made. (Genesis 2:1–3, NKJV)

According to the book of Genesis, God rested on the seventh day after finishing all of his creations. The seventh day doesn't give any suggestion that God requires a rest but rather can be a way of expressing that He had completed His work of creation. The only explanation to this is that God made this day for man as he blessed the day and sanctified it. There is no mentioning of the seventh day being finished. As we are on the last leg of our journey as to how the periodic table is the blueprint of the cosmos, it is amazing that elements of the seventh period and the group also fulfils the day's events.

Periodic Table (Seventh Period and Eighth Group) and Seventh Day of Genesis

Seventh Day: In Periods

The seventh day correlates to the seventh period, containing eighteen elements: francium (Fr), radium (Ra), actinium (Ac), rutherfordium (Rf), dubnium (Db), seaborgium (Sg), bohrium (Bh), hassium (Hs), meitnerium (Mt), darmstadtium (Ds), roentgenium (Rg), copernicium (Cn), Nihonium (Nh), flerovium (Fl), moscovium (Mc), livermorium (Lv), tennessine (Ts), and Oganesson (Og).With the exception of these elements, fourteen elements of the actinides are also considered in the seventh period, which include thorium (Th), protactinium (Pa), uranium (U), neptunium (Np), plutonium (Pu), americium (Am), curium (Cm), berkelium (Bk), californium (Cf), einsteinium (Es), fermium (Fm), mendelevium (Md), nobelium (No), and lawrencium (Lr). All of the elements of this group are radioactive and decay. One very interesting link to be found on the seventh day of creation and the periodic table is the "Trinity-mystery." It is important to remember the big bang originated with three elements: hydrogen, helium, and lithium. God is called the alpha and omega. Here we see three elements in the beginning of the universe and now we see three elements in the end of the periodic table. This confirms the Trinitarian nature of God. In the seventh period, only three elements—actinium (Ac), thorium Th), and uranium (U)— occur naturally while the remaining elements, are formed due to decaying of these "Trinitarian-elements.". Actinium glitters with a pale blue light in the dark because actinium ionises the surrounding air. It is naturally found only in traces in uranium ore. There are thirty-six radioisotopes of actinium identified; among them, Ac^{227} (21 years half-life), Ac^{225} (ten days half-life), and Ac^{226} (29 hours half-life) are the most stable. The remaining radioactive isotopes of actinium have half-lives that are less than few hours with the majority of these being less than one minute. They disintegrate with time, showing God's sacrificial nature. God sacrificed his Son for the sins of mankind. God abstained from showing up as the father in the history of mankind for giving the man the freedom to exercise his free will.

Seventh Day in Group

Group VIIIA is the last group of periodic table and also

links up with the seventh day of creation. According to Genesis, after finishing His creation, God rested and blessed the day. This is very closely linked with noble gas family (Zero Group) particularly because their outer shell is filled with electrons and becomes completely stable. These monatomic gases are odorless, colorless, and insoluble in water. The monoatomic gases or single atom gases of zero group (Group VIIIA) reminds us that there is only one God. The six noble gases that occur naturally are helium (He), neon (Ne), argon (Ar), krypton (Kr), xenon (Xe), and radon (Rn). These gases don't need to react with other elements in order to fill their outer shell. All of the noble gases have eight valence electrons except for helium, which has two. As a result, noble gases are extremely stable, and their outer shells are full. This stability of noble gases symbolizes the steadiness of God. Their odorless and colorless characteristics are a sign of God's invisible icon. It is a very interesting fact that earlier these elements were considered to be inert gases, but after making some simple as well as complex compounds of xenon, radon, and krypton, it has been confirmed that they simply possess incredibly low chemical reactivity. The reason for this low reactivity is the first ionization energy that decreases as size of the elements become large, their valence shell takes place further away from the nucleus, and electrons become easier to remove. The energy gained in creating xenon or radon fluoride is greater than the energy required for continuation of the reaction though these compounds are chemically stable.

As the seventh day marks the fulfilment of God's creation, similarly, elements of the last group also completely fills its electron becoming very stable in nature.

Days Conclusion

According to Genesis 2:2&3, God took rest on the seventh day from the creation process. He rests, indicating that the process of creation was stable. The period and the group that corresponds to Day 7 show two seemingly contradictory yet crucial attributes of God as described in the Scriptures. The elements within the period 7 are radioactive and disintegrate rapidly. This reminds us of the sacrificial nature of God and how He was willing to let Himself be disintegrated on the Cross for humanity. Now, the elements from Zero Group are all noble gases—indicating stable, full electron configurations. Similarly, this suggests the event of the seventh day—God's rest, which also can mean stability and the perfection or completion of creation. Everything is now complete and perfect. Again we see that the seventh day is as incomplete as the seventh period.

As we are in the image of God, we too are able to create new materials and expand His universe.

Periodic Trends Imitate Cross

In the periodic table, the identification of elements using groups and periods is similar to a Catholic priest making the cross in worship as the group trend moves from top to bottom in the groups and the periodic trend moves from left to right in the periods. The rules of chemistry for identification of the elements require a representation or a combination of both groups and periods. In this chapter, we discuss the group and periodic trends, which resemble the sign of a cross of Christ.

The Periodic Trends

In the periods, the elements are arranged in such a way that those with a similar number of shells of electrons belong to the same row. As we move across from group I to group II, this implies an increase in the number of electrons within the period. As the electrons increase within a period, the elements become less metallic, and the elements experience an increase in their atomic numbers. Each period begins with the alkali metals and finishes with the noble gases. In a period elements show a trend of decreasing atomic radius from left to right. The reason for this trend is that each successive new element has an added proton and electron, causing the electron to be drawn closer to the nucleus. A decrease in atomic radius also causes the ionization energy to increase when moving from left to right across a period. It is obvious that an element that is more tightly bound requires more energy to remove an electron. Similarly, in the case of electronegativity, it would increase as we move from left to right in the period because of the attraction that is exerted on the electrons by the nucleus.

Group Trends

Elements in the similar group have common characteristics.

For example, the reaction of alkali group elements sodium (Na) and potassium (K) with water and acid.

$$2Na+2H_2O \rightarrow 2NaOH +H_2$$
$$2K +2H_2O \rightarrow 2KOH+H_2$$

The above cited example shows they have the similar reactions with water forming hydroxide and hydrogen gas.

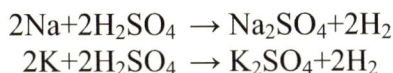

$$2Na+2H_2SO_4 \rightarrow Na_2SO_4+2H_2$$
$$2K+2H_2SO_4 \rightarrow K_2SO_4+2H_2$$

A reaction with the sulfuric acid (H_2SO_4) also forms similar by-products in the form of sulfate and hydrogen gas. It shows them having similar chemical reactions and thus has identical properties. Here we can see the reactivity increases as we go from Li (top) to Cs (bottom) in the first group.

Groups are considered the most important method of classifying the elements. Elements in the same group show increasing or decreasing patterns of atomic radius, ionization energy, electronegativity, etc. The atomic radii of the elements increase from top to bottom in a group.

A quantitative measure of the tendency of an element to lose electrons is given by its ionization enthalpy or energy The first ionization enthalpy generally increases as one goes across a period and decreases as one descends in a group.

A qualitative measure of the ability of an atom in a chemical compound to attract shared electrons is called electronegativity. Lower ionization energy is observed in each successive element from the top because it is easier to remove an electron since the atoms are less tightly bound. Similarly, in a group, we also see a top to the bottom decrease in electronegativity due to an increasing distance between valence electrons and the nucleus. *The p-block elements*: The p-block elements comprise those belonging to Group 13 to 18 (Group IIIA To Zero Group). The nonmetallic character increases as one moves from left to right across a period while metallic character increases as one goes down the group.

NORTH

Main Group Elements
1
IA

Main - Group Elements

18
VIIIA

1	2												13	14	15	16	17	1e
2	IIA												IIIA	IVA	VA	VIA	VIIA	

Transition Metals

3	4	5	6	7	8	9	10	11	12
IIIB	IVB	VB	VIB	VIIB		VIIIB		IB	IIB

Period

WEST

EAST

*Lanthanides
** Actinides

Ionization Energy: Largest toward NE of PT
Electron Affinity: Most favorable NE of PT
Atomic Radius: Largest toward SW corner of PT

SOUTH

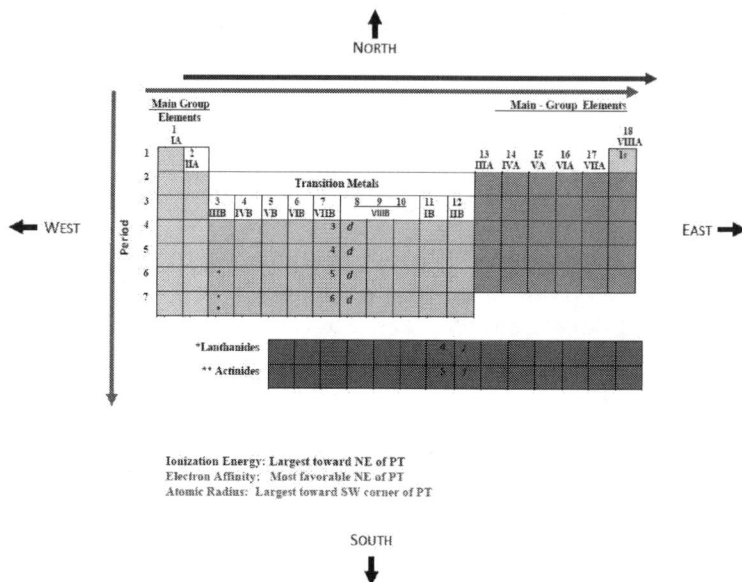

The periodic table trends exist in various forms but mainly imply that we move both horizontally and vertically just like a Catholic priest doing the sign of a cross. The major trends exist in the form of atomic radius, electronegativity, ionization energy, and electron affinity. Electron affinity and electronegativity both increase as we move along a period from left to right and decrease as we move from top to bottom in a group. Based on this, we can see that metallic character decreases while moving from left to right in a period and increases when we move from up to down a group in different periods. Therefore, it is possible to make a summary to remember these trends using a cross; we can imitate a Catholic priest making the sign of the cross. Thus, these periodic trends in periods and groups reminds us that the cross of Christ.

92

Adam and Eve

In the book of Genesis, there are two narrations regarding the creation of man. In the first narrative, Adam and Eve were created in God's image and were given instructions to multiply and be stewards over everything else that God had made. Now Adam was a particular man or a species. Atoms of the first row elements of the periodic table, after hydrogen and helium, differ from all other elements in one fundamental way: they are a homogeneous orbital. For example, both the 2s and 2p atomic orbitals of carbon are equally available for overlap with orbitals of some selected atoms while in silicon, the 3s orbital is contracted relative to 3p orbitals. This indicate that Adam represents the race *Homo sapiens*.

In the second part, we find descriptive narration of the process of creation and the division of sex.

> And the Lord God formed man of the dust of the ground, and breathed into his nostrils the breath of life; and man became a living soul. (Genesis 2:7)

> And the Lord God caused a deep sleep to fall upon Adam, and he slept: and he took one of his ribs, and closed up the flesh instead thereof; And the rib, which the Lord God had taken from man, made he a woman, and brought her unto the man And Adam said, This is now bone of my bones, and flesh of my flesh: she shall be

93

called Woman, because she was taken out of Man God fashions Adam from dust and places him in the Garden of Eden where he is to have dominion over the plants and animals. (Genesis 2:21–23)

The difference between man and woman is determined by hormones, specifically testosterone for men and estrogen for women. These hormones play a very vital part in maintaining bone mass. They are chemically very similar, made of similar elements, as testosterones chemical formula is $C_{19}H_{28}O_2$ and estrogen chemical composition is $C_{18}H_{24}O_2$. They look almost identical but differ in the number of carbon atoms. Removal of one carbon atom from testosterone to form estrogen parallels the removal of one rib from man to create woman.

Testosterone molecular formula: $C_{19}H_{28}O_2$
Molecular weight: 288.42442 g/mol
Estradiol molecular formula: $C_{18}H_{24}O_2$
Molecular weight: 272.38196 g/mol

Removing one carbon from testosterone will change it into estradiol, a primary female sex hormone, which is an estrogen.

Testosterone -1 carbon (4 hydrogen) = estradiol (estradiol is a form of estrogen)

288-(12 I 4) =272

We already know that the sixth day of creation is represented in the sixth period of the periodic table. In the sixth period, 7 "f" orbitals appear. The 7 true ribs in human also represents the 7 f orbitals. The f orbitals are inner orbitals as the ribs are found inside our body. Due to the f orbitals, we can see image elements in 6th period after Lanthanum, as in next 14 elements, new electron fills the

94

inner f orbitals and because of that, all these elements have similar properties like lanthanum. Bible says that God took one rib from Adam and made Eve. So Eve is also formed in the image of God as 7 rib represents the 7 "f" orbital. On Earth, we miss fourth lanthanide named promethium, which represents rib number 4, close to Adam's heart. It is funny to see the first love story of mankind in the periodic table.

Tree of the Knowledge

Nutrigenomics is a branch of science, which studies the interaction between genes and nutrition. Agouti mice are yellow in color, obese and prone to cancer and diabetes. These traits are passed to their offspring. As researchers in Duke University changed the mother's diet before conception, the agouti gene was turned off, and the new offspring do not have yellow fur. These new traits are passed to their offspring.

> And the Lord God commanded the man, saying, of every tree of the garden thou mayest freely eat: But of the tree of the knowledge of good and evil, thou shalt not eat of it: for in the day that thou eatest thereof thou shalt surely die. (Genesis 2:16–17)
>
> And when the woman saw that the tree was good for food and that it was pleasant to the eyes, and a tree to be desired to make one wise, she took of the fruit thereof, and did eat, and gave also unto her husband with her; and he did eat (Genesis 3:6)

Man is different from other living organisms as humans can attain and accumulate information and pass it on to other human beings.

This remarks the beginning of knowledge into the world. When Eve bit that forbidden fruit, mankind attained knowledge. Wisdom and knowledge are not at all bad things to attain. The disobedience of man brought sin into the world. Scripture tells us that knowledge is a gift from God. "For the Lord gives wisdom; from his mouth come knowledge and understanding" (Proverbs 2–6).

When the fruit of knowledge was consumed, the first point of contact was the tooth socket; there are four types of teeth, and thirty-two teeth in total. Knowledge entered the world with one man, created on the sixth day of creation. The sixth day of creation is related to the sixth period of the periodic table. This period also has four types of orbitals, and there are thirty-two elements, similar to the structure of the tooth socket.

> To the woman he said, "I will make your pains
> in childbearing very severe; with painful labour
> you will give birth to children. Your desire will
> be for your husband, and he will rule over you.
> (Genesis 3:16)

Now God says to Eve that after eating the fruit, her birth pain will increase. It is, natural to expect since Eve choose knowledge that means her baby needs a bigger brain and therefore a bigger head to accommodate all information to survive on earth. So the bigger head size will increase the birth pain as female pelvic inlet remained the same.

In women, pain increase sex hormones, which increases her attraction toward her man.

Eternal Life

Carbon

Carbon is a unique element because it forms numerous compounds that makes life possible on earth. The unique character of the carbon atom is due to its catenation, tetracovalency, and isomerism properties.

Furthermore, the unique character of the carbon is due to the simple harmonic motion of hydrogen in the first period of periodic system. The periodic system of elements is based on the simple idea of flat space-time. The groups represent time and the periods represent space and hydrogen represents the unit mass. The periodicity of the periodic system is produced by the simple harmonic motion of the hydrogen.

Suppose there is a hole in earth through its center. If we put an object in it, the object will display simple harmonic motion because gravity is zero at the center of the earth.

Now gravity is a manifestation of the curvature of space and time.

In the same way group IV is at the center of the periodic table that means for carbon, the effect of space-time curvature due to simple harmonic motion of hydrogen is zero or minimum. So carbon is capable to form infinite number of compounds. Thus carbon reminds us about infinite possibilities for living system.

Bismuth

Now sixth period also contains Bismuth whose atoms contain 83 protons and 126 neutrons. The nucleus of bismuth^{209} is in a higher energy state than the sum of the energies of a nucleus of thallium^{205} and an alpha particle (nucleus of helium^{4}). In quantum mechanics, whatever is not restricted by a conservation law can happen, and since alpha decay of bismuth^{209} to thallium^{205} does not violate conservation of energy or any other law, there is a possibility of alpha emission from Bismuth. In 2003, researchers at the Institut d'Astrophysique Spatiale in Orsay, France, reported the direct detection of alpha emission resulting from the decay of bismuth^{209} using a detector cooled to just two hundredths of a degree above absolute zero (20 mK) and calculate the half-life of bismuth^{209} to be 1.9×10^{19} years.

This is a long time kind of eternity as the universe is about fourteen billion years old and the half-life of bismuth^{209} is over a billion times longer than the current estimated age of the universe. This is a hint for us about eternity.

Bismuth also reminds us of our rebellious nature. Bismuth is the most diamagnetic of naturally occurring elements in the periodic table as diamagnetic metals create an induced magnetic field in a direction opposite to an externally applied magnetic field and are repelled by the applied magnetic field.

Bismuth crystals shows a rainbow of colors. This is the result of a thin oxide layer formation on its surface as spiral, stair-stepped structure which has a higher growth rate around the outside edges than on the inside edges. The variations in the thickness of the oxide layer that forms on

99

the surface of the crystal causes different wavelengths of light to interfere upon reflection, thus displaying a rainbow of colors. This rainbow of colors reminds us the covenant between God and Noah. The rainbow of color also reminds us the throne of God. The rainbow of color also reminds us His mercy in eternal life.

Rainbow also tells us that each person has an individual contract with God as each person sees a different rainbow due to location and movement of air that changes the refraction. Even if one person sees another person who seems "under" a rainbow, the second person will see a different rainbow—farther off—at the same angle as seen by the first person.

The seven colors of the rainbows remind us that the trinity of God is involved in this great show called life.

Trinity

We can see the trinity of God in the periodic table.

A) Hydrogen can be placed in three places:
   1) In the first group as hydrogen can donate an electron like sodium.
   2) In the fourth group as hydrogen can share an electron like carbon.
   3) In the seventh group as hydrogen can accept an electron like chlorine.

In this way, hydrogen, the first element of the periodic table can be placed in three places.

B) Then we see another group, the eighth group where three elements (Fe, Co, Ni) are placed in one group. Therefore, we can say that Fe is in 800, Co is in 080, and Ni is in 008 group to designate three elements in one group. We know that iron (Fe) is the cornerstone of the universe because iron (Fe) is the most stable element.

Iron is the last element of cooling process, and iron has the lowest energy level. Jesus came to the lowest place in the earth as a poor man.
Lowest place on the Earth:

1. Africa: Lake Asal, Djibouti:-156 meters below sea

level. (Minus 156 meters or 156 meters below sea level)

2. America, North: Death Valley, California, USA:86 meters below sea level. (Minus 86 meters or 86 meters below sea level)
3. America, South: Laguna del Carbón, Argentina:-105 meters below sea level. (Minus 105 meters or 105 meters below sea level)
4. Asia: Dead Sea shore, Israel:-418 meters below sea level. (Minus 418 meters or 418 meters below sea level)
5. Australia: Lake Eyre, South Australia:-12 meters below sea level. (Minus 12 meters or 12 meters below sea level)
6. Europe: Caspian Sea shore, Russia: -28 meters below sea level. (Minus 28 meters or 28 meters below sea level)

Jesus was born in Israel because it is the lowest place on earth. In all the continents of the earth, the Dead Sea shore is the lowest place on the earth. Now we can understand that why God asked Abraham to go to the west from Iraq because God wants to meet the man in the lowest place of earth. Another reason is that Canaan is the land of a curse as Noah cursed his grandson, Canaan. Jesus came to the land of a curse, Canaan, to take our curse away.

Here in the periodic table, we can see one element in three places and three elements in one place. Now in Revelation 1:8, Jesus says I am the Alpha and the Omega. The numerical value of Alpha is 1 and the numerical value of Omega is 800. Element number 1 (hydrogen) can be placed in *three* positions. Element number 800 (Iron) is one among *three* elements in the eighth group. Thus, we see a similar pattern in Creator and Creation.

Above statements, remind us what St. Paul says in Roman 1:20,

> For since the creation of world God's invisible qualities—his eternal power and divine nature—have been clearly seen, being understood from what has been made, so that men are without excuse.

C) According to the big bang theory, only three elements were created in the beginning. These elements are hydrogen, helium, and lithium.

D) The Bible in Genesis 1:1–5 says that there was darkness in the beginning and God created light on the first day. We can interpret this situation in mathematics by giving 0 to explain darkness and 1 to explain light as the absence of light is darkness. In mathematics, this system is called as the binary system.

In binary system:

1 is represented as 1
2 is represented as 10
3 is represented as 11
4 is represented as 100
5 is represented as 101
6 is represented as 110
7 is represented as 111

God blessed the seventh day (Genesis 2:3) because seven shows 111 or the trinity of God. The chemical element number 7 is nitrogen. Nitrogen has three single electrons (111) in its three P-orbitals.

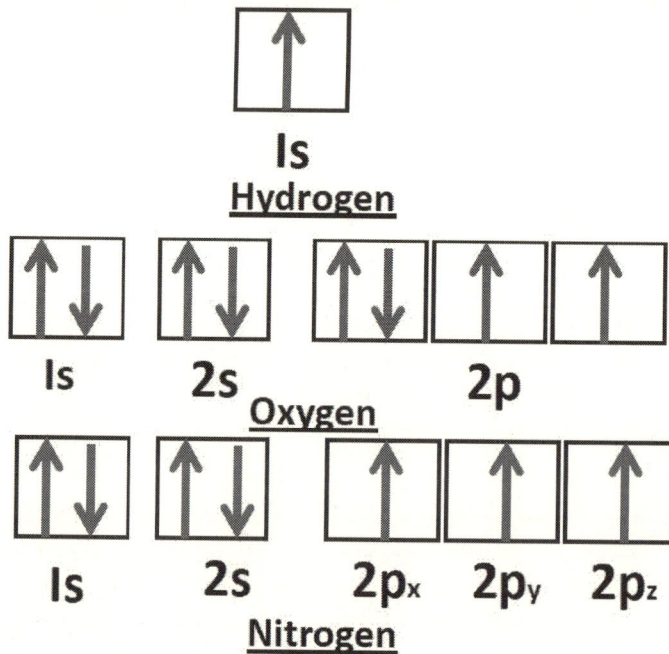

Is
Hydrogen

Is   **2s**   **2p**

Oxygen

Is   **2s**   **2p$_x$**   **2p$_y$**   **2p$_z$**

Nitrogen

Nitrogen is not reactive even though it has three single electrons. Hydrogen has a single electron in its s-orbital and oxygen has two single electrons in its outer p-orbital and these two elements are highly reactive. The mysterious inactivity of nitrogen indicates that God was inactive on the seventh day.

The following is a list of the sevens and their multiples in the creation story of Genesis:

- 35 times God is found. (7x5)
- 7 times "On the Earth (Hebrew only)" is found.
- 21 times "Earth, earth, or land" is found. (7x3)
- 7 times "heaven(s), sky (excluding 'heavenly sky')" are found.
- 7 times "Good" is found.

104

- 7 times "Water(s) (beneath the heavens)" are found.
- 7 times "flying, fly, or birds" are found.
- 7 times "crawls, walks, and land animals" are found.
- 14 times "day or days" are found. (7x2)

All these seven reminds us that 111 or triune God created this universe.

It is well known that there are seven continents on the earth. God is present in all these seven continents with a symbol of seven burning lamps with fire, showing the majesty of his Holy Spirit. The number 7 is extremely important in the Bible because it is used many times compared to other numbers. In the march around Jericho, they marched for seven days and seven times on the seventh day. There were seven priests and seven trumpets. Seven has many more meanings as well. There are seven days in the week, seven notes on the musical scale, seven directions (left, right, up, down, forward, back, and center), etc. Thus, seven is the supernatural number of the natural world indicating the presence of triune God.

Human Soul

Dimensional analysis provides a strategy for choosing relevant data and its presentation. If it is possible to identify the factors involved in a physical situation, dimensional analysis can form a relationship between them. The resulting expressions may not at look rigorous but these qualitative results converted to quantitative forms can be used to obtain any unknown factors from experimental analysis.

Dimensions and Units

Carl Friedrich Gauss (1777–1855) and Wilhelm Eduard Weber (1804–1891) had reduced all units, which became necessary during their work in electricity and magnetism to the units of length, mass, and time. Any physical situation can be described by length, mass, and time. These are all known as dimensions.

Of course, dimensions are of no use without a magnitude being attached. We must know more than that something has a length. It must also have a standardized unit, such as a meter, a foot, a yard, etc. Dimensions are properties, which can be measured. Units are the standard elements we use to quantify these dimensions. In the dimensional analysis, we are only concerned with the nature of the dimension, i.e. its quality, not its quantity. The following common abbreviation is used:

Length = L
Mass = M
Time = T

In this section, we are only concerned with M, L, and T. We can represent all the physical properties we are interested in with M, L, and T. Some quantities have no dimensions. For example, the sine of an angle is defined as the ratio of the lengths of two particular sides of a triangle. Thus, the dimensions of the sine are L/L, or 1. Therefore, the sine function is "dimensionless." The many other examples of "dimensionless" quantities are:

1. All trigonometric functions
2. Exponential functions
3. Logarithms

106

4. Angles
5. Quantities such as the number of people in the room
6. Numbers (like 2, 61552; etc.)

The following table lists dimensions of some common physical quantities:

Quantity	SI Unit		Dimension
Velocity	m/s	ms^{-1}	$[L][T]^{-1}$
Acceleration	m/s²	ms^{-2}	$[L][T]^{-2}$
Force	Kg m/s²	$Kg\ ms^{-2}$	$[M][L][T]^{-2}$
Energy	Kg m²/s²	$Kg\ m^2s^{-2}$	$[M][L]^2[T]^{-2}$
Pressure	Kg/m/s²	$Kgm^{-1}s^{-2}$	$[M][L]^{-1}[T]^{-2}$
Density	Kg/m³	$Kg\ m^{-3}$	$[M][L]^{-3}$

In other words E → P x V.
$$ML^2T^{-2} = ML^{-1}T^{-2} \times L^3$$

We know that volume V is expressed as L^3 and pressure P is expressed as $ML^{-1}T^{-2}$.

So energy E is expressed as ML^2T^{-2}.

Thus, we can have a definite volume or size even after our physical death because energy is everlasting.

Now it is very interesting to see that in Chemistry E = P x V is the Gas Equation in Dimensional Analysis as PV = nRT and n and R are constant whereas temperature is an objective comparative measurement of heat or energy. Heat is expressed as ML^2T^{-2}.

Bible says in Genesis 2:7 that God instilled gas into the nostrils of man and man became a living soul. Bible shows the connection of Gas and Soul. And the Lord God formed man of the dust of the ground, and breathed into his nostrils the breath of life, and man became a living soul. (Gen 2:7)

107

Bible also says that when Jesus will come again in the clouds, we will meet Him in the air. It also connects that concept of energy to a soul.

Conclusion

God is the creator of our world. As we know, the book of Genesis is the first book of the Hebrew Bible and the Christian Old Testament, which means the Book of Beginnings. It is the first book of the Law of Moses, or Torah, consisting of the first five books of the Bible. There are many new beginnings recorded in Genesis, but it all starts with the creation of the world. There are seven days of creation recorded in the beginning of Genesis, but the Hebrew word *yom* simply means "a period of time with a beginning and an ending."

Earth is made up of eighty-nine elements. These elements were classified in the periodic table. There are striking similarities between the periodic table and the first chapter of Genesis. The story of the universe is the story of the elements, which is also the story of creation. In the periodic table, there are groups and periods; in the Bible, there are evenings and mornings. Genesis is a story of the beginning of the great human family, and the periodic table starts with the alkali family.

God

On the first day of creation, according to Genesis 1:2, it is written that the Spirit of God was hovering over the waters. Similarly, hydrogen is the first element of the universe, the first element of the first period, and whose atomic number is one, imitates that motion. Hydrogen has only one electron, so it can donate electrons like lithium, a first group element, or it can share electron like carbon, a fourth group element, or it can accept electrons like fluorine, the seventh group element. So hydrogen can be considered in simple harmonic motion in the first period. In this way, one element can be placed in three different groups, showing the relationship of one God in three persons.

First Day

In Genesis 1:3, on the first day, God created light. The first period has hydrogen and helium. In stars, hydrogen fuses to form helium and this process creates light. In another word, stars obtained their energy from the nuclear fusion of hydrogen to form helium. Similarly, in the first group, there are lithium, sodium, potassium, rubidium, caesium, and francium are called alkali metals. When alkali metals, like sodium, come into contact with water, heat and light are produced. No wonder our oceans are filled with sodium in the form of common salt.

Second Day

The second day of creation, God separated the water above from the water below as recorded in Genesis 1:6. In the periodic table, we see a huge, substantial gap between the second and third groups, or Group IIA and Group IIIA.The large gap mirrors the second day's great division. In the second day, God created the atmosphere. The second period contains nitrogen and oxygen, which are major constituents 98% of our atmosphere.

Third Day

As stated in Genesis 1:11, God created plants on the third day. As we already know, the second day is shown by groups IIA and IIIA, so the third day will be shown by Group IVA Group IVA contains carbon, the backbone of all plants. Magnesium, which is found in the third period, is the central element of chlorophyll. It is chlorophyll that gives plants their green color.

Fourth Day

In Genesis1:14, the fourth day, God created the sun, moon, and stars. Iron (Fe) is the most well-known element in period 4, being the most common metal in the sun and stars. Iron-56 has the lowest energy density of any isotope of any element, meaning that it is the most massive element that can be produced in supergiant stars. In addition, we see a new energy level or d orbital emerging in the fourth period. The corresponding group for the fourth day is Group VA. This group also contains phosphorus, a shining element.

Fifth Day

On the fifth day as said in Genesis 1:20, God created birds of the air and fish of the sea. Fish and birds both have nucleated red blood cells, which carry oxygen. In that sense, birds and fish can be grouped together. Moreover, fish and birds, including dinosaurs, had unidirectional oxygen intake. The next group (Group VIA) includes oxygen, the element needed for life.

Sixth Day

On the sixth day as recorded in Genesis 1:26, God created man in His own image. In the sixth period and in the third group (reflecting the Trinity), there is lanthanum. Lanthanum has fourteen image elements. These image elements are formed because electrons go to inner orbitals instead of outer orbitals. This indicates that the godly image is an inner image, not an outer image. It is wonderful to see that there are seven f orbitals corresponding to the verse in the book of Revelation 4:5, stating that God has seven Spirits. The Bible's descriptions match 100 percent with nature and science. Group VIIA halogens form diatomic molecules (X_2 where X refers to a halogen atom) when they are in their pure states. The bonds in these diatomic molecules are nonpolar covalent single bonds. The peculiar nature of halogen supports the sixth-day creation because God made pairs of each of the higher animals, including human beings, as male and female.

Seventh Day

On the seventh day, God rested from His work. The last group of the periodic table is called the zero group elements or the noble gasses. Due to the fact that their outer shells are full, these elements are in a constant state of rest, the way God rested on the seventh day. In the Bible, the seventh day is the only day that is not closed. In the same way, the seventh period of the periodic table is an open period even though man filled the period with the synthetic elements. These elements are not stable, as many of them exist in the lab for less than a minute, keeping the period an open one.

Periodic Table and Prophecy

When Mendeleev discovered the periodic table, he left some blocks empty, and he predicted the discovery of new elements. He even predicted and named many of the elements to be discovered later as Eka-silicon. In the same way, the Bible contains prophecies which are fulfilled as time rolls on.

Periodic Table and Tree of Knowledge

When Eve bit that forbidden fruit, sin started. If we look at the tooth socket, there are four types of teeth with thirtytwo in total. Likewise, in the sixth period of the periodic table, there are four types of orbital and a total of thirtytwo

113

elements.

The periodic table shows the deep connection with Genesis. According to Genesis, eight acts of creation were done over six days following a conclusion. In each of the first three days, three different acts of separation were done, such as in the first day the darkness from light, the second day the "waters above" from the "waters below," and the third day the sea from the land. So these three days of creation are called separation days. The first three periods of the periodic table are also showing the gaps between the groups, which confirm the separation. In each of the next three days, these previous divisions were settled with nonliving and living creations. In the fourth day, the darkness and light settled with the sun, moon, and stars, and on the fifth day, the seas and skies settled with the fishes and birds.

Finally, on the sixth day, land-based creatures and mankind settled on the land.

General Similarities

If we look in the Bible, we can see that the human race started with two people. In the first period, there are two elements. Then the Great Flood occurred, and eight people came out from the ship. In the second period, we see eight elements. Then a new race is born by the name of Israel; Jacob, his four wives, his twelve sons, and one daughter, making eighteen people. Also, we see eighteen elements in the next level of the periodic table. The elements were there, and the classification of the elements was there; predicting the beginning of human race by two people, looking for a perfect generation by eight people, looking for a new race by eighteen people. Finally, the highest period in the periodic table has thirty-two elements including lanthanum and the lanthanides, indicating that man as a whole is created in the image of God. Elements existed before the human race. All of these elements are talking only one story, and this story talked not only of two people, not only of eight people, not only of eighteen people, but of humanity in whole and its first sin and the God and His salvation plan. Man artificially synthesized new elements confirming the statement of Genesis 1:26 that man is the image of the creator.

Correlations and links between elements of the periodic table and day-wise creations of God are not just a coincidence. There is definitely something more to it. Elements are the construct of all living and nonliving things and are the common language of the universe. Similarly, the periodic table is the base of all elements that occur in the universe. The book of Genesis is a divine universal story of creation and is incomplete without the elements. These underlying correlations with the periodic table give us a better understanding of how God relates things. Everything in the universe works under laws of nature, which are established by the spirit of God.

As the universe is made up of elements, so any story of the universe is confined to the elements. Chemistry is the central science, and the periodic table is its icon. The Periodic table of elements is the blueprint of the universe and so the creation story of the universe in the Bible is also encrypted within it, proclaiming the legitimacy of the story. This encryption could have been only attained with the help of a deity. Hence, the final conclusion is reached that the periodic table is the blueprint of the universe and is analogous to God's creation.

Bibliography

Abrol, Y. P. and Ahmad A. Sulphur in Plants. Kluwer
   Academic Publishers, Dordrecht, 2003. ISBN 1-
   40201247-0.

Abumrad, N. N. (1984). "Molybdenum—is it an
   essential trace metal?" *Bulletin of the New York
   Academy of Medicine* 60 (2): 163–71. PMC 1911702.
   PMID 6426561.

McLeish, Andrew. *Geological Science.* 2nd ed. Thomas
   Nelson & Sons, 1992. p. 122. ISBN 0-17-448221-3.

Atkins, P. W., and J. De Paula. *Elements of Physical
   Chemistry.* Oxford: Oxford University Press, 2013.

Atzeni, S. and J. Meyer-ter-Vehn. "Nuclear Fusion
   Reactions," in *The Physics of Inertial Fusion.*
   University of Oxford Press, 2004. ISBN 978-0-19-
   856264-1

Bandstra, Barry L. *Reading the Old Testament: An
   Introduction to the Hebrew Bible.* Wadsworth
   Publishing Company, 1999. ISBN 0-495-39105-0.

Barnes, Richard Stephen Kent. *The Invertebrates: A
   Synthesis.* Wiley-Blackwell, 2001: p. 3. ISBN 978-0-
   63204761-1.

Barrett, J. "Atomic Structure and Periodicity." Royal
   Society of Chemistry, London, 2002.

Bautista, Manuel A. and Anil K. Pradhan. "Iron and Nickel Abundances in H~II Regions and Supernova Remnants." *Bulletin of the American Astronomical Society*27 (1995): 865. Bibcode 1995AAS...186.3707B

Beckett, M. A. and A. W. G. Platt. "The Periodic Table at a Glance," Blackwell, London, UK, 2006.

Campbell, Neil A., Brad Williamson, and Robin J. Heyden. *Biology: Exploring Life*. Boston, Massachusetts: Pearson Prentice Hall, 2006. ISBN 0-13-250882-6.

Chang, R., and K. A. Goldsby. *Chemistry*. New York: McGraw-Hill, 2013.

Connelly, Neil G., et al. "Elements." *Nomenclature of Inorganic Chemistry*. London: Royal Society of Chemistry, 2005. ISBN 0-85404-438-8.

Cotton, F. A., G. Wilkinson, C. A. Murillo, and M. Bochmann. "Advanced Inorganic Chemistry." 6th ed. Wiley/ Interscience, NY, 1999.

Cox, P. A. *The Elements: Their Origin, Abundance, and Distribution*, Oxford University Press, Oxford, UK, 1989.

Crichton, R. R. "Biological Inorganic Chemistry: An," Elsevier, NY, 2007.

Cstonyl. J., et al. "Anaerobic Respiration on Tellurate and Other Metalloids in Bacteria from Hydrothermal Vent Fields in the Eastern Pacific Ocean." *Applied and Environmental Microbiology*—72 (7) 4950-4956.

Dean, ed. *Lange's Handbook of Chemistry*. 15th ed., online version, McGraw-Hill, 1999; Section 4, Table

4.1 Electronic Configuration and Properties of the Elements. (Elements 1–103)

Dingle, Adrian. *The Periodic Table*. New York: Kingfisher, 2007.

Emsley, J. W. "The Elements." 3rd ed. Oxford University Press, NY, 1998.

Enemark, John H. *et al.* (2004). "Synthetic Analogues and Reaction Systems Relevant to the Molybdenum and Tungsten Oxotransferases." *Chem. Rev.* 104 (2): 1175–1200. doi:10.1021/cr020609d. PMID 14871153

Enghag, P. "Encyclopedia of the Elements," Wiley-VCH, Weinheim. 2004. ISBN 3-527-30666-8.

Epstein E. The anomaly of silicon in plant biology. Proc. Natl. Acad. Sci. USA, 1994. 91:11–17.

Epstein E. (1999). *Silicon.* Annual Review of Plant Physiology and Plant Molecular Biology50,641–*664*.

Fortey R. *Life: A Natural History of the First Four Billion Years of Life on Earth*. New York, US: Random House, 1997.

Frausto da Silva, J. J. R. and R. J. P. Williams. *The Biological Chemistry of the Elements*. Oxford University Press, 1991.

Furgang, A. "The Noble Gases: He, Ne, Ar, Kr, Xe, Rn." Rosen Publishing Group, Inc., NY, 2010.

Gray, Theodore. *The Elements: A Visual Exploration of Every Known Atom in the Universe*. New York: Black Dog & Leventhal Publishers, 2009. ISBN 978-1-57912-814-2.

Greenwood, N. N. and A. Earnshaw. Chemistry of the Elements, Butterworth-Heinemann, Oxford. Pergamon Press, 2001. ISBN: 0-7506-3365-4.

Ham, Becky. *The Periodic Table*. New York: Chelsea House, 2008.

Harris, P. "The composition of the earth." In Gass, I. G. *et al*, eds. *Understanding the Earth: A Reader in the Earth Sciences*. Horsham: Artemis Press for the Open University Press, 1972. ISBN 0-85141-308-0.

Herndon, J. M. (2005). "Scientific basis of knowledge on Earth's composition." *Current Science* 88 (7): 1034–1037.

Housecroft, C. E. and A. G. Sharpe. "Inorganic Chemistry." 3rd ed. Pearson/Prentice Hall, NY, 2008. http://bible.cc/genesis/1-1.htm http://www.genesis.net.au/~bible/kjv/genesis/ Calvin, J. Genesis. (Grand Rapids: Eerdmans, 1948) 78–79.

Kocsis, M. G., K. D. Nolte, D. Rhodes, T. L. Shen, D. A. Gage, and A. D. Hanson. 1998. Dimethylsulfoniopropionate biosynthesis in Spartina alterniflora1. Evidence that S-methylmethionine and dimethylsulfoniopropylamine are intermediates. Plant Physiol. 117 (1):273-81.

Kopp, G. and J. Lean. 2011. "A new, lower value of total solar irradiance: Evidence and climate significance." *Geophys. Res. Lett.*: L01706. Bibcode 2011GeoRL… 3801706K. doi:10.1029/2010GL045777.

Krebs, Robert E. *The History and Use of Our Earth's Chemical Elements: A Reference Guide*. Westport, Conn.: Greenwood Press, 2006. pp. 47–50. ISBN 0-

313-33438-2.

Kvam, Kristen E., Linda S. Schearing, Valarie H. Ziegler, eds. (1999). *Eve and Adam: Jewish, Christian, and Muslim readings on Genesis and gender*. Indiana University Press. pp. 515. ISBN 0-253-21271-5.

Levi, P., and R. Posenthal. *The Periodic Table*. Camberwell, Vic.: Penguin, 2010.

Lide, D. R., ed. *CRC Handbook of Chemistry and Physics*. 86th ed. Boca Raton, FL: CRC Press, 2005. ISBN 0-8493-0486-5.

Lodish, H., A. Berk, P. Matsudaira, C. A. Kaiser, M. Krieger, M. P. Scott, S. L. Zipurksy, J. Darnell. *Molecular Cell Biology*. 5th ed. New York, New York: WH Freeman and Company, 2004.

Marschner, H. Mineral Nutrition of Higher Plants. San Diego: Academic Press, 1995. Beneficial Mineral Elements; pp. 405–435.

Masterson, William and Cecile Hurley. *Chemistry: Principles and Reactions*. 6th ed. Belmont, CA: Brooks/Cole Cengage Learning, 2009. pp. 24–42. ISBN 978-0-49512671-3.

McHenry, H. M. "Human Evolution." In *Evolution: The First Four Billion Years*, edited by Michael Rusc and Joseph Travis. Cambridge, Massachusetts: The Belknap Press of Harvard University Press, 2009. p. 265. ISBN 978-0-674-03175-3.

Measures, C. I., and J. M. Edmond. 1982. Beryllium in the water column of the central North Pacific. Nature 297:51–53. doi:10.1038/297051a0.

Measures, C. I., T. L. Ku, S. Luo, J. R. Southon, X. Xu, and M. Kusakabe. 1996. The distribution of 10Be and 9Be in the South Atlantic. Deep-Sea Res. 43:987–1009.

Miessler, G. L., and D. A. Tarr. *Inorganic Chemistry*. 3rd ed. Pearson Prentice Hall: Upper Saddle River, NJ, USA, 2004.

Noonan, J. P. (2010). "Neanderthal genomics and the evolution of modern humans." *Genome Res.* 20 (5): 547–53. doi:10.1101/gr.076000.108. PMC 2860157. PMID 20439435.

Pearcy, W. and E. Krygier. Biological transport of zinc-65 into the deep sea. Limnology and Oceanography, 1977.

Penland, J. "Dietary boron, brain function, and cognitive performance." *Environmental Health Perspectives*—1994 Nov; 102 Suppl. 7:65-72. 1994.

Puddephatt, R. J. and P. K. Monaghan. "Periodic Table of the Elements." 2nd ed. Oxford University Press, NY, 1986.

Rinnosuke, Fukai and W. Meinke. Trace analysis of marine organ-isms: A comparison of activation analysis and conventional methods. Limnology and Oceanography, Vol. 4, 1959.

Scerri, E. R. *The Periodic Table: Its Story and Its Significance*. Oxford University Press, 2007. ISBN 978-0-19530573-9.

Schnug, E. *Sulfur in Agroecosystems*. Kluwer Academic Publishers, 1998. ISBN 0-7923-5123-1.

Schrauzer, G. and K. Shrestha. "Lithium in drinking

water and the incidences of crimes, suicides, and arrests related to drug addictions." *Biol Trace Elem Res*, 25 (2):105-13. 1990.

Shriver, D. F. and P. W. Atkins. *Inorganic Chemistry.* 3rd. Ed. Oxford University Press, 1999. ISBN 0-19-850330-X.

Stwertka, A. *A Guide to the Elements.* New York: Oxford University Press, USA, 2012. Haines, Tim and Paul Chambers. *The Complete Guide to Prehistoric Life.* Firefly Books, 2005.

Towner, Wayne Sibley. *Genesis.* Westminster John Knox Press, 2001.

Waggoner, Ben. "Vertebrates: Fossil Record." UCMP, 2011. http://www.ucmp.berkeley.Edu/vertebrates/vertfr.html.

Wollack, Edward J. "Cosmology: The Study of the Universe." *Universe 101: Big Bang Theory.* NASA, 2010. Retrieved 27 April 2011.

Wood, Bernard. 1987. "Who is the 'real' *Homo habilis*?" *Nature* 327 (6119): 187–188. doi:10.1038/327187a0. PMID 3106828.

Made in the USA
Columbia, SC
23 May 2024

36122653R00074